DIRECTIONS IN DEVELOPMENT

Nurturing Development

Aid and Cooperation in Today's Changing World

Ismail Serageldin

The World Bank
Washington, D.C.

©1995 The International Bank for Reconstruction
and Development/THE WORLD BANK
1818 H Street, N.W.
Washington, D.C. 20433

Cover photograph: teacher with two students, Bhutan; by Curt Carnemark for
the World Bank.

Library of Congress Cataloging-in-Publication Data

Serageldin, Ismail, 1944–
      Nurturing development : aid and cooperation in today's changing
  world / Ismail Serageldin.
          p.   cm. — (Directions in development)
      Includes bibliographical references.
      ISBN 0-8213-3184-1
      1. Economic assistance—Developing countries.   2. Developing
  countries—Economic policy.   3. International cooperation.
  I. Title.   II. Series : Directions in development (Washington, D.C.)
  HC60.S4275   1995
  338.9'1'091724—dc20   95-6432
                                                                          CIP

Development is like a tree:
it can be nurtured in its growth only by feeding its roots,
not by pulling on its branches.

Contents

Foreword

As the World Bank celebrates its fiftieth anniversary, we are reminded of how much progress the development effort has made over the last several decades. But we are also reminded just how great the task ahead is, if hunger is to be abolished and the poor equipped to improve quality of life for themselves and their children.

This book draws on the lessons of over four decades of development experience and points the way ahead for the international aid community in the coming decade. The richly textured presentation is less sharply etched than the recent World Bank "vision" paper, *Learning from the Past, Embracing the Future*, but is fully compatible with it. Indeed, running throughout the many vignettes and sections of this short book, one finds the same five major challenges that were articulated in that paper: pursuing economic reforms to enhance growth and reduce poverty, investing in people, protecting the environment, stimulating the private sector, and supporting good governance. Linking these themes is what Ismail Serageldin describes as "nurturing development"—an apt title drawing on the metaphor of the tree that cannot be made to grow by pulling on its branches, but only by feeding its roots.

The decade ahead will see doubts raised in many quarters about the the need for aid. Let there be no doubt. It is needed. But we must focus on the effectiveness with which it is dispensed. It should be nurturing to the people of the developing countries—who are the ultimate means and ends of all development.

Lewis T. Preston
President
The World Bank

Preface

The world is changing at an amazing pace. The Soviet Union is no more. The cold war, which paralyzed the international community in its grip for over forty years, is over. Centrally planned economies are recognized as failures. The power of markets is not only recognized and lauded but sometimes endowed with seemingly magical properties.[1]

Yet, far from witnessing the "end of history"[2] with the inevitable victory of democratic institutions and free-market economies, the emerging post–cold war world is a troubling place. Ethnic strife is rampant. The transition to economic liberalism is proving exceptionally arduous. The rich of the world are getting richer, and the poor, poorer.

Many use this last point to pillory the efforts of development assistance over the last half century. Others see these developments in a different light and value the contributions of aid and development assistance. This essay is a contribution to that debate.

Today, an increasing number of people both in the North (donor countries) and the South (recipient countries) are questioning the purposes, effectiveness, and results of close to half a century of "foreign aid." The range of motivations among the questioners is vast. In the North they go from populist politicians who say, "Let's spend the money on internal problems at home"—to criticisms founded on either efficiency or effectiveness of aid as a tool for promoting development in the recipient country or in promoting the national interests of the donor country (however defined)—to the moral outrage felt by many over the persistent images of famine in Africa "after all this aid."

---

1. See Ismail Serageldin, "Public Administration in the 1990s: Rising to the Challenge," in *Public Administration in the Nineties: Trends and Innovations, Proceeding of the XXIInd International Congress of Administrative Sciences* (Brussels: International Institute of Administrative Sciences, 1992).

2. See Francis Fukuyama, *The End of History and the Last Man* (New York: Free Press, 1992).

In the South, the collapse of communism, and the more general disfavor with which socialism is now viewed, has spawned a new generation of post–cold war critics of aid. These critics range from disgruntled academics and politicians who see in it a smoke screen to divert attention from the inequities of global distribution of wealth, resulting in an ever-richer North—to those who decry the infringement on sovereignty that conditions on aid bring—to those who want other types of conditions attached to the aid—to those who see aid as a sop thrown to the developing world while the North, in fact, recoups it all in exports of goods and services.

Professionals in the national and international agencies concerned with the promotion of development have not helped matters much. The public views them as overpaid, slothful bureaucrats whose main concerns are petty turf wars and the perpetuation of their empires. With rare exceptions, they have largely failed to convince the public of the importance of their mission, of the intricacies of the tasks with which they are entrusted, or of the effectiveness with which they are actually discharging these responsibilities.

This essay, contributed by one of those who have dedicated their lives to promoting development in the poorer part of the world, intends to make the case that aid is a necessary, although by no means decisive, and certainly not sufficient, element in accelerating development and improving the well-being of hundreds of millions of people in the world today. In making this case the author is hopeful that a number of popular misconceptions about aid and development will be laid to rest. Parts of this material were published by the Swedish International Development Authority (SIDA) in 1993 and in various journals. But the material is presented here, in this shortened format, to make it more readily accessible.

The essay is divided into four parts. The first deals with the changing world context in which the debate is currently taking place. The second is a review of the arguments against aid and their rebuttal, the third part deals with the lessons learned from four decades of international development assistance. The final section deals with where we go from here.

Threaded throughout the text are the same five themes set out in *The World Bank Group: Learning from the Past, Embracing the Future,* a document issued on the occasion of the Bank's fiftieth anniversary. These themes are continuing economic reform, human resource development, environment and sustainability, private sector development, and good governance.

The future of the developing countries will be determined primarily by the people of those countries. It is their determination, commitment, and vision that must create the new world where poverty will retreat and the basic well-being of the people, all the people, will make the needed gains to ensure to each the basic minimum that we all take for granted. Yet, a well-targeted and judicious investment in their efforts will accelerate the process and help those who would help themselves.

The manner in which this assistance is provided is essential to its effectiveness. It must be based on a real sense of partnership, not on a donor-recipient mentality. Experience shows that only those programs that are truly "owned" by the developing countries have a chance of sustained success. Such programs must therefore be "nurtured" through dialogue, mutual respect, and understanding. Development programs cannot be forced and they cannot be imposed from the outside, no matter how noble the motivations of those who would wish to impose their point of view. These programs must also be "nurturing"—encouraging private initiative, empowering the weak and the marginalized, and promoting a vibrant civil society, all key in promoting sustainable development. It is therefore apt that this book should be called *Nurturing Development.* In both senses of the words, it captures what we are trying to do at the World Bank as we face the challenges of today and tomorrow.

Ismail Serageldin
Vice President, Environmentally Sustainable Development
The World Bank

Acknowledgments

This essay was written to present a personal point of view, an unabashed advocacy of the value and importance of development aid and cooperation in a rapidly changing world. Much of the material presented here draws on the work of many scholars and institutions. To each one of them I am most grateful. In particular, I asked a large number of my colleagues to review, check, and comment on particular sections that fall within their areas of expertise. The completion of this essay thus received tremendous support and assistance from many, many people. I would like to specifically thank the following:

Shankar Acharya, Martha Ainsworth, Ibrahim Al-Assaf, Nicole Ball, Edgardo Barandiaran, Les Barker, Bruce Benton, Eveling Bermudez, Inger Bertilsson, Kim Bieler, Hans Binswanger, Carlston Boucher, Lily Bran, Loup Brefort, Ron Brigish, Michael Bruno, Silvio Capoluongo, Leif Christoffersen, John Clark, Kevin Cleaver, Cynthia Cook, Ernest Corea, Marie Laure Cossa, Audrey Cox, Robert Crown, Therese Cruz, Timothy Cullen, Meta de Coquereaumont, Tekola Dejene, Louis DeMerode, Lionel Demery, Mamadou Dia, Jean Doyen, Jean-Luc Dubois, Betty Dvorscak, Mai Eidi, Ed Elmendorf, Claire Evans, Francois Falloux, Habib Fetini, Joe Gadek, Maria Cristina Germany, Paul Gleason, Rosetta Grimm, Christiaan Grootaert, Benjamin Gyepi-Garbrah, Teresa Hartnett, Ian Heggie, Edward Heneveld, Richard Herbert, Barbara Herz, Alicia Hetzner, Herbert Howe, Ishrat Husain, Ishrat Z. Husain, Sarwat Hussain, Kwang Jun, Sarah Keener, Hilary Kiell, Sara Kim, Pierre Landell-Mills, Jeri Larson, Janet Leno, Frank Mancino, Kris Martin, Malonga Miatudila, Said Mikhail, Peter Moock, Jeanne Moore, Elizabeth Morris-Hughes, Leila N'Diaye, Michel Noel, Catherine Oram,

Erskine Pickwick, Yvonne Playfair-Scott, Jean Ponchamni, David Pyle, Nimrod Raphaeli, Farida Reza, Gerard Rice, John Riverson, Kathy Rosen, Maryam Salim, Lawrence Salmen, Sheryl Sandberg, Rene San Martin, Miguel Schloss, Aissatou Seck, Jim Shafer, Alexander Shakow, Ibrahim Shihata, Hector Sierra, Jerry Silverman, Roy Stacy, Andrew Steer, Mai Stewart, Roger Sullivan, Lawrence Summers, Fernando Tonolete, Moctar Toure, Nicholas Van Praag, Adriaan Verspoor, Alexander Von Der Osten, Cynthia Villanueva, Sadek Wahba, Harry Walters, and Aubrey Williams.

I would like to particularly thank Heather Imboden, who prepared this monograph for publication.

Needless to say, I alone bear the responsibility of all errors and weaknesses in this essay. The views expressed herein are my own and should not be attributed to the World Bank or to any of its affiliated organizations or their member governments.

1. A Changing World

The World Setting

The end of the cold war brought new hopes that the dream of a new, just, and equitable world order could be finally set up under international law and buttressed by the collective will of all humanity to cooperate and collaborate.[1] This naive hope was quickly shattered. The short-lived triumphalism, epitomized by Fukuyama's slogan "the end of history,"[2] was seen to be hollow. The collapse of the USSR did not lead to instant democracy, peace, and happiness. Indeed, the world of the post–cold war era is a menacing place. True, the specter of nuclear holocaust has receded. In its place, however, intrastate and interstate ethnic tensions and murderous conflicts. Death and misery are no less real to their victims for being localized.

For a brief moment, the Earth Summit in Rio cast its spell. Here was the whole community of nations and the peoples of the earth proclaiming their common humanity, their interdependence as passengers on and co-stewards of Spaceship Earth. Yet Rio was only a milestone on the path toward this expanded consciousness. Much remains to be done to build more lasting structures on the spirit of Rio, or, better still, to infuse the existing institutions with the spirit of Rio. What are the obstacles to this manifestation of our common humanity?

Contradictory Tendencies

The present situation is exceptionally complex. Contradictory tendencies seem to be acting. On the one hand, the forces of globalization and homogenization are definitely at work. On the other hand, the assertion of specificity—ethnic, religious, or cultural—is also powerfully present in almost all societies.

The most powerful of the forces of globalization are clearly the increasing interdependence of the world's national economies and the integration of the financial and telecommunications markets as never before. A trillion dollars are transacted daily in the financial markets. Revenues from telecommunications in the OECD countries alone increased from $225 billion in 1980 to over $365 billion in 1990.

The markets have arguably been running ahead of the capacity of national governments to understand them, much less regulate them. New types of financial instruments and services and the rapid emergence of markets in such services are forcing a reassessment of the appropriate role of national governments and institutions in promoting the welfare of citizens. They are also showing how permeable the political boundaries that divide the sovereign nation-states have become to the ethereal commerce of ideas and funds that travel through the airwaves.

A second forceful presence for the increased global consciousness is the environmental movement, which seeks to remind all humans that they are stewards of this earth. Although the environmental problems tend to be felt by the public in terms of immediate local issues, much progress has been made on increasing awareness of the global issues such as global warming, the ozone layer, and biodiversity.

A third powerful force that was significantly strengthened by the end of the cold war is the universal drive for the respect of human rights, and its closely associated set of concerns with the nature of the democratic process. Superpower rivalry in the developing world is no longer an excuse for either side to support tyrants who have little support among their people, as was routinely done over the past 40 years. This has allowed, for the first time, the local forces in practically every society to assert themselves, seeking greater voice and greater power. The downside of this phenomenon is the emergence of hateful, petty nationalisms that transform the rightful call for identity and participation into a call for hating your neighbor and ultimately even "ethnic cleansing."

A related and powerful aspect of the drive for human rights is the rise of feminism and gender consciousness. An essential ingredient of any true conception of human rights is that these must apply to all human beings. Women have been and continue to be oppressed in most societies today and that is an intolerable injustice that must be remedied. Furthermore, as is so frequently the case with any form of discrimination, there is ample evidence that all of society, not just the victimized minority, would greatly benefit from the emancipation of the oppressed and their empowerment to be all that they can be.

A fourth and related force for globalization, one that links up to the previous three, is the emergence of a new phenomenon that I would like to refer to as the international civil society. We have long known, and now Robert Putnam of Harvard University has empirically demonstrated based on data from Italy,[3] that the civil society is central to the promotion of good governance at the national level. Indeed, that complex web of interactive organizations is key to maintaining responsive government and protecting individual freedoms. Today, the emergence of truly global telecommunications, the increased awareness of international issues such as the environment, and the unremitting drive for the general acceptance of respect for human rights everywhere have all combined to create a new international civil society through such organizations as Amnesty International, Greenpeace, and the Red Cross, which not only have branches everywhere but also actively communicate through an increasingly dense network of such institutions that bring solidarity and support to one another's causes.

What are the forces of disintegration relying on? They are actively growing because as the citizens of the world face the large, the new, the unknown, they feel profoundly insecure. There is none of the optimism that once placed unbounded confidence in technology, and there is very real cynicism in many countries about the political system's ability to create utopia. In a word, there is a growing sense of unpredictability about the future. Under these circumstances, people tend to regress: if the future cannot be clearly defined as the goal, one lives for the present. If the present is troublesome and disconcerting, one falls back onto the past. The past here means one's ethnic, religious, cultural, or national roots. It is a drawing closer of the circle within which one can feel secure, a regression to the concept of tribe and clan.

In every society, there is a class, which can be loosely called the intelligentsia, that includes intellectuals, academics, artists, opinion makers, and role models and fashions for each member in that society mirrors in which they see themselves and windows through which they see the world. The mirrors can show a person as a member of an oppressed minority, as the invincible executor of a manifest destiny, or as the instrument of God on earth. The windows can show a hostile world full of conspirators and enemies, or they can show a world full of opportunities and promise. It is this combination of mirrors and windows that defines the boundaries of the mind, the boundaries that define where the "us" ends and the "them" begins.[4]

Clearly, these boundaries of the mind change depending on the issue at hand, but the crisscrossing lines of cleavage in a society are created in this fashion. Crisis or great tension can cause a break in these societies, usually along a dominant fault line created by such a cleavage. This explains the splits in the former Yugoslavia, or that between Czechs and Slovaks, while Switzerland, for its part, succeeds in maintaining a Swiss identity without sacrificing the tremendous diversity of its many localisms.

Yet are there no common themes in the forces of globalization and in the problems shared by humanity to forge a common set of beliefs and values based on things that most people agree about, such as free markets, democracy, and human rights? Is there the making of a global ideological revolution here? Not quite. For although there is a simple, seductive view that the world is moving to adopt free markets as an organizing economic principle, democracy as an organizing political principle, human rights as the basic value for organizing a system of beliefs, and environment as a program for action; this view does not address the complexities inherent in such thematic constructs, nor their interactions.

There is no doubt that these general principles are present in much of the public debate everywhere in the world today. They are undoubtedly constituent elements of the evolving world consciousness. For many in the developing world this set of constructs has been seen as "Western," usually meaning originally European values, currently championed by the United States and Europe. They fear the spread of these ideas as "Westernization," which they see as the adoption—forced or voluntary—of Western values and institutions by the rest of the world, thereby sealing the hegemony of the Western powers by the most complete subjugation of all peoples and societies of the world; a subjugation that ensures their adherence as marginal members of the Western world order. This view is possibly the reflection of the insecurities that lead people to seek refuge in the narrow constructs of the past. Perhaps the solution to all these problems and contradictions is to carry these ideas further, much further than Western societies have dared to do until now, and in the process create that global world order that would be truly new and truly universal.

Principles of Universal Appeal

Let's look at these constituent elements and just how Western they really are. Human rights is an idea of universal appeal. Its most persistent current formulations are international declarations and instruments, universally adopted and ratified even if initiated and driven by Western governments and citizens' groups. These rights have become the inalienable rights of all people everywhere by virtue of being alive. Of course much more remains to be done to give real meaning and substance to such universal statements. Women and minorities continue to suffer in most societies. Furthermore, with over 1 billion people going hungry every day, and the highly selective application of various UN sanctions or interventions, many feel that there is a certain hollow ring to the universal declaration of human rights and the more recent instruments all the way to the declaration of Vienna of 1993.[5] There is a certain hypocrisy in a world system that recognizes the rights of citizens if they are on one side of that imaginary line we call a political frontier but not if they are on the other, and then claims to adhere to the universality of these basic rights.

Reliance on markets, however, is not an ideological construct as much as a pragmatic adoption of what works. It was the failure of the centrally planned economies that led to the almost universal adoption of a free market stance in most countries. True, some ideologues are trying to elevate free markets to the level of ideology and to urge the elimination of government and the privatization of everything in sight. But most reasonable people do not adopt such extreme positions. They recognize that the ruthless efficiency of the market must be tempered by the compassion of a caring and nurturing government, much as justice must be tempered by mercy to be more than legalism. Furthermore, the needs of the public in terms of health, security, and environmental protection will require a degree of regulation and control and standard setting, even if pragmatically one would rely on incentives and markets to obtain the desired results.

Somewhere between the level of universal construct (human rights) and the pragmatic workable solution (free markets) lies the difficult question of democracy. In its most generally understood sense, democracy is taken to mean multiparty political processes relying on periodic elections by universal suffrage. That is considered to be the Western model of political organization, and arguably the only proven model for protection against abuses of human rights. But it leaves many questions unanswered as it straddles principle and pragmatism. There is nothing inherently Western or nonuniversal about it, especially if the pragmatic elements are emphasized to suit better the unique features of each society. After all, there is tremendous variety among the different Western countries themselves, even among the European countries. The systems of the United States, Germany, France, the United Kingdom, and Switzerland are profoundly different, yet they all are democratic societies.

Here it is pertinent to recall the importance of the role of the civil society as guarantor of good governance nationally, and the concomitant rise of the still embryonic international civil society of international movements and networks of nongovernmental organizations (NGOs). These may be the seeds of an enriched international environment in which diversity of experiences is seen not as deviation from a normative ideal but as the multiple manifestation of the application of universal principles to local realities.

As for the environment as the basis for a universal political program, that is manifestly inadequate. That environmental consciousness should permeate all decisions, and that the objective should be to promote sustainable development, is not in question. But the range of problems confronting human societies today transcends that eminently acceptable environmental formulation.

The Heart of the Problem

The powerful and inspiring principles that have such universal appeal must become the driving force of the new world order to which all of humanity aspires. These principles must govern individual behavior and international behavior. Sadly, behavior that would never be condoned between individuals seems to be tolerated between nations, as if the legal construct of the nation-state somehow insulates the people who live within its confines from the effects of the actions undertaken at the international level between nations.

Why is such a simple approach not being followed? Because behind all the rhetoric is a profound crisis of values. If racism is universally condemned, its reverse, accepting that all people are really and truly intrinsically equal in their rights, is not practiced.

The world today is divided more by wealth and well-being than by politics. The citizens of the rich countries are concerned about protecting their life-style and living standards and worried about potential migration of the poor into their societies.[6] In some parts of the rich societies, concern with immigration has become a potent political issue. The more "liberal" use it to argue for aid as a means of keeping the poor at home. The more xenophobic or racist forms of political interpretation are raising the specter of the "browning of the West" at the very time that many in the poor countries are concerned about the "Westernization" of the world. This paradox does not stand up to rational analysis. Most voluntary migration is beneficial to both migrant and host country.

The bulk of migration in the world today is involuntary. And whether it is the result of wars and natural disasters or of new building and infrastructure, it is mostly happening in the developing countries. The World Bank has recently estimated that as many as 10 million people are being involuntarily displaced annually in the developing countries as a result of infrastructure projects associated with urban growth and rural dams. This is not to deny that there is a significant demand for migration to the rich countries of the North in search of economic opportunities. The poor, who risk their lives in small craft whether from Haiti or (earlier) from Viet Nam, bear witness to the needs and aspirations of the deprived on this planet. Such images on the TV screens of Northern sitting rooms, however, tend to lump together all the developing countries as one mass of undifferentiated suffering humanity. This view must be nuanced.

The poor developing countries are not all the same. Many are doing well in improving their living standards, but many others, representing the poorest fifth of humanity, are falling further behind in almost every aspect of socioeconomic endeavor. The tremendous achievements of most of the developing countries must not be underestimated, but the problems confronting the poorest 20 to 25 percent of the citizens of this planet cannot be ignored.

Consider These Facts

• The richest 20 percent of the world's population receive 83 percent of its income. The poorest 20 percent receive 1.4 percent! Thirty years ago that rich group (approximately corresponding to the OECD) was already 30 times as rich as the poorest 20 percent. Today they are 60 times as rich.

• There is a 25-year gap in life expectancy at birth between the poorest countries and Europe.

• Infant mortality is eight times higher in the poorest countries than it is in Europe (117 vs. 14 deaths before the age of one per 1,000 live births).

• Maternal mortality rates in Africa are 50 times as high as they are in Europe (500 vs. 10 deaths per 100,000 live births).

• Fewer than one in five girls go to school in Mali and Niger, compared with almost 100 percent in Europe.

Taken in the aggregate, such indicators are associated with a level of misery and degradation that is beneath any definition of human decency:

  • Over 1 billion people live on less than one dollar a day.
  • Over 800 million people go hungry every day.
  • Over 2 billion people are suffering from either hunger or malnutrition with severe health impacts.
  • Over 40,000 hunger-related deaths occur each day.
  • One out of three children in the developing world is under nourished.

Environmentally, although the OECD countries account for the bulk of global pollution, basic conditions are far worse in the developing world:

  • Over 1 billion people do not have access to clean water.
  • Over 1.7 billion people do not have access to sanitation.
  • Over 1.3 billion people suffer from unhealthy levels of air pollution, mostly in the big cities.
  • Over 700 million women and children suffer from indoor air pollution due to biomass-burning stoves that is equivalent to smoking three packs of cigarettes a day.
  • Hundreds of millions of poor farmers have difficulty maintaining the fertility of the soils from which they eke out a meager living.

And to that stock of suffering humanity close to 90 million people are added every year—more than the population of unified Germany. To give that demographic its true dimensions, consider this comparison between Europe and Sub-Saharan Africa (SSA): in 1950 the population of SSA was half that of Europe; by 1985 SSA's population equaled Europe's. By 2025 SSA's population will be three times Europe's.

The technological gap, like the income gap, is also growing. As we move from the machine age to the knowledge age, the control of the vast information networks and the superb research and development facilities in the North give the OECD countries a tremendous advantage.

An educational gap reinforces the technological gap. There is a vast and growing gap between the North and the South in the production and availability of scientists and engineers (3,800 per million population in the North compared to less than 200 in the South, as of 1989).[7] Of equal concern is the qualitative gap, as many of the institutions of science and technology in the South are deprived of equipment and supplies and voided of their standards of excellence in the service of political expediency and cronyism. The South is still struggling with the needs of basic laboratory equipment at a time when the North is mainstreaming computers for the average person to use as simply as telephones, when technology is truly finding its way into every home, putting unrivaled power and speed literally in the hands of millions. This knowledge gap is becoming serious, for, unlike the skills gap, inequities in incomes will be exacerbated by the disparities in knowledge in the knowledge-based world of tomorrow. The differences in the incomes between the best and worst computer programmers exceed by many multiples those between the best and worst welders or plumbers. And the knowledge-based industries are being fed by an explosion of information unmatched in history.

In the United States alone, there are 14,000 magazines published for the general public. There are over 55,000 trade books published annually: that is one book every 10 minutes, not counting the specialized journals and scientific books! The Library of Congress doubles its holdings every 14 years and, at the rate things are going, will soon double them every 7 years. In some fields, such as environmental management in developing countries, the number of publications doubles every 18 months. Over 70 percent of the references in the World Bank's *World Development Report 1992* dealing with development and the environment were less than two years old.

Matching this information explosion is the explosion in computing and communications. Some 50 million computers were sold worldwide in 1993 at about $1,500 per unit. Many of these PCs are more powerful than the mainframe computers of a generation ago!

And things are set for even more radical changes over the next decade. Early in the new century we can expect that the CPUs of 16 Cray YMP computers costing $320 million today will be replaced by a single microchip costing about $100. Such a microchip would contain the equivalent of 1 billion transistors, compared with 20 million today for cutting edge technology.

Even more important, is the trend toward networking. In the United States, which prefigures the rest of the world, we have seen the proportion of computers hooked into networks rise from 10 to 60 percent between 1989 and 1993![8]

The Aid Debate in Context

This then is the context in which the debate about aid is being carried out in the world today. The North, the rich countries of the OECD, are considering their own domestic problems, concerned about their budgetary stringencies. They are turning inward and away from internationalism or multilateralism. Commercial interests have replaced the cold war as the dominant elements in the formulation of foreign policy. Political leaders find little support for expanding the effort to assist the less fortunate in the world from an electorate that is concerned with its own unemployment, welfare, and the social security of an aging population. The appeal to common humanity resonates with only a small minority of the population, driven by idealistic considerations.

The desire to cut official development assistance (ODA) flows is also being supported by two separate currents from two very different "camps." First are the isolationists, who see no reason to exert themselves for countries that became geopolitically irrelevant with the end of the cold war. They find all sorts of excuses to argue that ODA funding is misplaced and should be redirected to domestic and commercial ends. Second are those who genuinely want to help the poor and the needy but believe that the current international system is not able to do the job effectively and efficiently and seek a new paradigm. The various motivations and arguments have become intertwined, and this requires sorting out the essential arguments about aid and the development paradigm. This essay is intended as a contribution to that debate.

The rest of the essay is organized in three parts. First is a review, and a rebuttal, of the most common arguments against aid. While fully acknowledging the enormous task that remains, especially with an exploding world population, it nevertheless sets the record straight as to the enormous achievements of the developing countries as a whole in the last generation. Again, it must be remembered that while the situation is becoming increasingly problematic for that bottom quintile of the world's population, the middle 60 percent has seen considerable improvement, by any socioeconomic indicator, over the past four decades.

Second is a long review of what has been learned over the past forty years about what works and what has not worked in the development assistance field. Third, and last, is a brief "envoi" as to where to go from here.

2. Foreign Aid
and Economic Development

Foreign aid is defined as foreign assistance provided by governments (bilateral assistance) or international agencies (multilateral assistance). International agencies include international financial institutions (IFIs) such as the World Bank, as well as the United Nations (UN) agencies, such as UNESCO and the Food and Agriculture Organization (FAO), and the UN programs, such as the United Nations Development Programme (UNDP) and United Nations Children's Fund (UNICEF). Foreign aid can take the form of direct grant transfer of funds, technical assistance, or loans under concessional terms.

Aid became a significant part of industrial countries' foreign policy after World War II, spearheaded initially by the Marshall Plan to assist in the reconstruction of Europe. Soon, with decolonization and prosperity returning to the industrial countries, most of the Organization for Economic Cooperation and Development (OECD) members became aid givers.[9] OECD's Development Assistance Committee (DAC) reported that from 1962 to 1990 DAC contributions to developing countries, in constant 1987 dollars and excluding contributions to international financial organizations, increased almost 150 percent— from $15.1 billion in 1962 to $37 billion in 1990.[10] However, as a percentage of GNP, DAC aid on average fell from 0.5 percent in 1962 to 0.35 percent in 1990.[11] The variation among DAC member countries is, however, significant: from a high of 1.17 percent (1990) of GNP for Norway to a low of 0.21 percent (1990) for the United States.[12]

Several issues related to foreign aid have generated a body of literature.[13] These issues can be divided in two broad groups: the motivation for aid and the effectiveness of aid in achieving greater welfare of people in the recipient country. The bulk of our concerns in this essay is with the latter. Nevertheless, it is important to recognize that in many donor countries political issues, especially during the cold war, were behind the support for aid. Political motives have not been universal, however. The motivation for aid has ranged from pure altruism—that is, concern for the poor and for correcting unequal distribution of income, especially due to a lack of natural resources—to the pursuit of national objectives, such as national security and commercial benefit.[14] Although some studies have shown that bilateral aid tends to be driven by the donor's perceived national interests rather than by humanitarian needs or what the developing countries perceive as their economic needs,[15] as Eaton states, "Once multilateral aid is taken into account there is more evidence that the recipients' needs are an issue."[16]

The Arguments against Aid

Leaving aside questions of motivation, arguments against the effectiveness of aid can be grouped broadly under four headings:

• *Aid has failed* and does not contribute to promoting development—the result of four decades of well-intentioned assistance is continued misery and backwardness.

• *Aid promotes dependency* in the recipient countries, which never succeed in relying on themselves.

• *Aid is misused*, going to the rich elite and corrupt rulers, not to the needy in the recipient countries.

• *Trade is better than aid* in promoting economic growth.

It is not surprising to find many opponents of aid using all of these arguments, or variants thereof, in addition to motivational and political aspects, in making their case against aid. For example, P. T. Bauer suggests that the motivation for aid (and a consequence) has been to create a North-South confrontation.[17] As Bauer and Yamey state, "The foreign aid that created [the Third World] did not originate in pressure from the Third World, but rather was introduced and organized by the West. Thus by foreign aid did the West create a Third World, and one hostile in itself."[18]

The criticism of aid to developing countries also comes from radical economists who see aid as a form of dependency, promoting repressive regimes that survive thanks to foreign assistance. In this respect classical economists have some common ground with left-sympathizing economists.

This is by no means the total case against development aid as it exists. Many aid practitioners, including this author, have many complaints about the frustrations encountered in being more effective in discharging our responsibilities. These will constitute the bulk of this essay. Nevertheless, the summary statements of Bauer and Yamey and others are feeding the negative public perceptions of development aid because their assessments do not give a balanced picture. Because these four general arguments against aid are encountered like a leitmotiv in all public discussions of development aid, they will be addressed at the outset of this essay.

Rebuttal of the Arguments against Aid

Again, rebutting the four general arguments against aid does not mean that there are not many other problems with the mechanisms, instruments, and processes of development assistance as it is presently practiced. These will be taken up at length later in this essay.

Aid Has Failed

The single most potent argument advanced by those who claim that "aid has failed" is the continuing poverty of the developing countries and their presumed lackluster economic performance "in spite of massive aid." This is the first canard that should be laid to rest.

• In the last four decades the developing countries, as a group, have performed better than the OECD countries. They have held their own in per capita income growth rate over the period 1953 to 1988 although they had higher population growth rates (figure 2-1).

• The *best performers* among the developing countries (figure 2-2) significantly outperformed the best historical performances among the OECD industrial countries. It is striking to note that, just as Olympic records are improving all the time, the new economic champions are going farther, faster, and from a lower base than the old champions. Thus, the Republic of Korea doubled its output per person in only 11 years (1966 to 1977), compared to 58 years for the United Kingdom (1780 to 1838), 47 years for the United States (1839 to 1886), and 34 years for Japan (1885 to 1919).

• The developing countries' performance on the *social* front far outdistances anything known in the history of the OECD industrial countries. In the clean, wholesome environments of today's Northern

Figure 2-1. Per Capita Output Growth in the OECD and Developing Countries and Significant World Events, 1953–88

Per capita output growth (percent; five-year moving average)

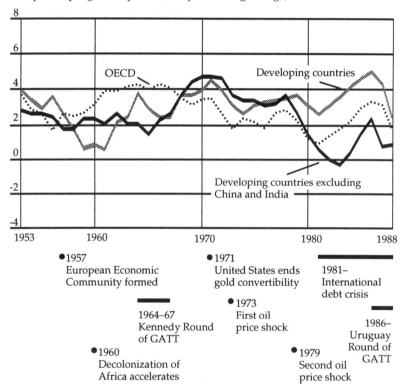

Source: World Bank, *World Development Report 1991: The Challenge of Development* (New York: Oxford University Press, 1991), 17.

democratic Europe, the vivid images of Charles Dickens and the misery of workers in the nineteenth and early twentieth centuries are too easily forgotten. In contrast to the developed nations, in which economic transformation invariably *preceded* social improvements, the developing countries are laboring at both economic and social transformation simultaneously. A few statistics eloquently make the case:

- Life expectancy went up from 41 years in 1950 to 58 years in 1990, based on 90 low- and lower-middle-income countries with populations of more than 500,000.
- Illiteracy (as a percentage of the population 15 years or older) was reduced from 39 percent in 1970 to 29 percent in 1985.
- Gross enrollments in primary education as a percentage of the 6–11 age group went up from 78 percent in 1965 to 105 percent in 1990.[19]
- Access to safe water, limited to about one-quarter of the developing countries' total population in the late 1960s, is now

Figure 2-2. Periods during which Output per Person Doubled, Selected Countries

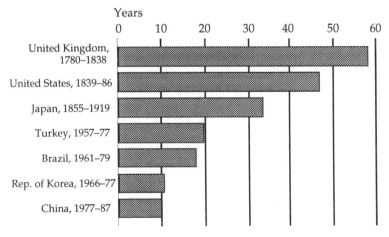

Source: World Bank, *World Development Report 1991: The Challenge of Development* (New York: Oxford University Press, 1991), 12.

available to about two-thirds of the vastly larger developing-
country population of today.

- Child immunization, launched by UNICEF in 1974, when
fewer than 5 percent of the children in developing countries
were immunized, in 1990 protected 78 percent from measles,

Box 2-1. The Relentless Battle against Disease

Much has been done . . .

The developing countries have waged a largely successful battle
against many of the killer diseases once considered endemic in
many countries:
- *Smallpox:* Smallpox, which until recently was a dreadful killer
with case-fatality ranging from 20 to 40 percent, has been eradicated by an impressive international effort. No case has been reported
since one case that occurred in October 1977 in Somalia and the two
accidental cases that occurred in Birmingham, Alabama, in August
and September 1978. The worldwide eradication was confirmed by
the WHO Assembly in May 1980.
- *Yaws:* Some forty years ago there were about 100 million active
cases of this parasitic disease in the developing countries. The mass
treatment campaigns organized in the 1960s have resulted in substantial reduction of yaws prevalence in all previously affected
areas, including Africa, South America, Asia, and the western
Pacific. Currently, yaws afflicts fewer than 3 million persons in the
world, and its distribution is patchy and confined to small localities
in West and Central Africa, Indonesia, and Papua New Guinea.
- *Onchocerciasis:* Until recently, experts estimated that more than
20 million people, mostly in Africa and Central America, were suffering from onchocerciasis. A titanic and continuous effort was
made in the last twenty years to control this disease. This effort has
spectacularly reduced the prevalence of infection in the young age
group (less than fifteen years of age) in the seven West African
countries in the Volta River basin.
- *Malaria:* No accurate data are available regarding the incidence
of malaria in the developing economies. However, there is a universal agreement that this disease remains the most important infec-
tious disease in the world. The advent of insecticides in the 1940s

82 percent from polio, and 88 percent from tuberculosis.
- Diseases that used to be endemic, claiming tens of millions of lives, have been controlled, even though more remains to be done (box 2-1).

But how much has aid contributed to this overall improved per-

---

made it possible to organize massive malaria eradication campaigns in the 1950s and 1960s. These activities markedly decreased the incidence of malaria in many parts of the world. Malaria has been totally eradicated in Europe and in some developing economies, such as Taiwan (China) and Cuba.

- *Trypanosomiasis (sleeping sickness):* From the 1880s to the 1940s African trypanosomiasis, commonly known as sleeping sickness, played a major role in both morbidity and mortality in most of Sub-Saharan Africa. From the late 1950s to the mid-1960s control campaigns were responsible for the significant decrease in incidence and prevalence of the disease, even in large countries such as Zaire.

. . . but so much still remains

- *Trypanosomiasis (sleeping sickness):* Due to various socioeconomic problems, many areas that have experienced significant reduction in sleeping sickness cases are now experiencing a resurgence of the disease. Chagas disease, the American variation of trypanosomiasis, is still endemic in many parts of South America.
- *Life expectancy:* Despite major improvements in the last four decades (albeit with wide variations among countries and regions), there is a difference of twenty-five years between the least developed countries and the most developed countries.
- *Infant mortality rates:* There is still an eightfold gap between the least advanced and the most advanced countries (117 deaths before the age of one per 1,000 live births compared with 14 per 1,000).
- *Maternal mortality rates:* Available data show that maternal mortality rates have not improved in many developing countries, in which the level frequently exceeds 500 deaths per 100,000 live births, as compared to 10 per 100,000 in developed countries. The reasons why women die are many and include both technical and administrative causes.

formance? There have been attempts to analyze the gains and losses
for both the donor and the recipient due to aid.[20] Thus, some empiri-
cal evidence is available to answer the question—does aid work?

Cassen and others[21] and Krueger and others[22] have provided the
most comprehensive evaluations of foreign aid. The major conclusion of the Cassen report is that the contribution of aid to economic
growth and development depends on the country and the period
being studied as well as the methods used for measurement and
evaluation of the aid programs. Cassen suggests that, overall, aid
has been beneficial to growth if one excludes food aid. This contra-
dicts earlier studies by Mosley and others[23] which suggest that aid
has had no effect on increasing growth rates. Krueger and others
provide a less positive view than Cassen, but the Cassen report
argues convincingly that aid has helped reduce poverty although,
again, the results depend on individual countries and individual
projects.[24] The reason that the findings of such global surveys
appear cautious is that much of international bilateral aid during the
cold war was politically motivated and, unlike multilateral aid, was
not focused on promoting development objectives. This is now
changing. The arguments on the *effectiveness* of aid and how to
increase the *efficiency* of aid management are the core of the remain-
der of this essay.

Aid Promotes Dependency

That aid *necessarily* promotes dependency is demonstrably false.
Economies like Taiwan (China) and Korea have received substantial
amounts of aid but today are economic powerhouses in their own
right.

While the case of dependency may arise in specific countries at
specific times, this premise is not convincing on a global basis.
Today, except in Sub-Saharan Africa, aid represents such a small
percentage of GNP that to talk of "dependency" is ludicrous. The
aid received by Latin America, East Asia, and South Asia represents
only 0.4 percent, 0.7 percent, and 1.7 percent of their respective
GNPs. Even if all the assistance promised to Eastern Europe and the

Commonwealth of Independent States (CIS) materialized, it would represent only 2 percent of GNP.[25] Such small amounts are clearly regional averages and mask significant differences by country. Nevertheless, they are indicative. As for Sub-Saharan Africa, where ODA flows in 1992 were close to 10 percent of GNP, the present approach to providing aid is being geared more and more toward building capacity and increasing financial self-reliance.

Aid Is Misused

There is much truth to this criticism, especially when politically motivated bilateral aid was used to support "friendly regimes" in the cold war era. This misuse was exacerbated by the lack of transparency of budgets or accountability of governments among the recipient countries. Prominent critics such as Bauer and Yamey observed:

> Foreign aid does not go to the pitiable figures we see on aid posters or in aid advertisements—it goes to their rulers. The policies of these rulers who receive aid are sometimes directly responsible for conditions such as those depicted. This is notably so in parts of Africa and Southeast Asia. But even where this is not so, the policies of the rulers, including their patterns of public spending, are determined by their own personal and political interests, among which the position of the poorest has very low priority. . . .
>
> These anomalies or paradoxes are obscured when it is suggested that giving money to the rulers of poor countries is the same thing as giving it to poor, even destitute people. Giving money to governments is certainly not the same thing as helping the poor. [26]

This issue was pushed to the fore of World Bank concerns under the general heading of "governance." Among the mainstream development agencies the issue was first joined in 1989 with the publication of the World Bank's long-term perspective study, *Sub-Saharan*

Africa: From Crisis to Sustainable Growth.[27] Much more has been done since then.[28]

Suffice it to say at this point that whether aid has reached the poor is still a matter of controversy. Although Cassen attempts to show a direct linkage between aid and poverty alleviation,[29] in many countries, aid, especially politically motivated bilateral aid, has been diverted from its original objectives and has failed to reach the poorest groups of society. Increased awareness of the political dimensions of aid has led many agencies to openly criticize governments and attach political conditionalities to aid disbursement.[30] There has been a move toward a greater role for nongovernmental organizations in the use of foreign assistance.[31]

Aid versus Trade

Some have argued that removing trade barriers would transfer about $54 billion to the developing countries annually, approximately equivalent to the total annual official development assistance from the OECD countries.[32] Hence, trade instead of aid would help everyone: OECD consumers would get cheaper goods, OECD taxes could be used domestically (or reduced), and the developing countries would receive the same amount as before.

This argument is simplistic. The approximately $50 billion that freer trade would bring to developing economies would be highly concentrated among a few economies: Korea, Mexico, Singapore, or Taiwan (China). It would not go to Chad, Ethiopia, or Zambia.

No, what is needed is *both* trade and aid.

The Problems of Aid

This is not to say that there are no problems with the present scope, mechanisms, or effectiveness of aid. Many problems impede better use of foreign assistance. Among these are a lack of coordination on the part of the donor agencies, unsustainable aid programs, poor evaluation of programs that prevents learning from experiences,[33] and the difficulty of reaching the poorest groups because most aid is channeled through government institutions. This is not all; much has been learned over the years about what needs to be done differently. Among these lessons is the necessity of looking at the total country performance (not just individual projects) as the basis of assessment, with special emphasis on developing human resources; using sound macroeconomic policies; keeping development focused on reducing poverty; coupling development with environmental sustainability; educating women and accelerating positive change by making use of their de facto central role in all development-related activities; ensuring civil rights and promoting good governance anchored in a robust civil society; using a human-centered, market-friendly policy framework; promoting the private sector within an enabling environment, and building local capacity; moving toward a better balance between public and private investment; understanding that reform is a long-term battle waged on many fronts; and carefully evaluating, and hopefully reducing, military expenditures. All of these issues are taken up in the next chapter.

Cassen found that within a donor nation diversity of aid activities, while desirable, could also hamper the cohesiveness of that country's aid program.[34] In many cases there has been duplication of effort. The demand of each national donor agency for its own budgetary, procurement, and accounting procedures as well as other requirements has put tremendous pressure on the management capacities of many recipient countries.

These and similar issues of donor coordination and recipient capacity raised in the Cassen report have to a certain extent been tackled through the creation of "Consultative Groups" (CGs) and "roundtables" for each recipient country. The programs of assistance increasingly are geared to the specific needs of the recipient countries. But certainly much more needs to be done to strengthen overall aid coordination as well as national management capacity in recipient countries.

To understand why coordination continues to be a major problem, we need to survey the many different actors in the field of international development assistance in addition to the different kinds of aid being proffered to promote development in the developing countries.[35] The recent statement of the secretary general of the UN, entitled "An Agenda for Development,"[36] sets out a comprehensive framework for the UN system to help.

Beyond the UN system, the entire international development community is now reaching a consensus that aid is most efficiently utilized by countries that are committed to poverty reduction through environmentally sustainable development, have strong institutions, and manage their economies soundly in fiscal and monetary terms. Proper governance, sound budgetary procedures, and an enabling environment for private investment and the civil society are part of the evolving reality of the developing countries that use aid most effectively. Donors, for their part, must ensure that their own policies and procedures reinforce such trends.

A learning process is occurring, and it is reasonable to suppose that steady progress can be made in improving the effectiveness of aid. With the end of the cold war, donors can more readily focus on the developmental dimension of aid unfettered by concerns of global politics or national security. This is a new opportunity to make a major step forward in the relations between the developed and developing countries.

3. What We Have Learned

It is always tempting to try to reduce the most important lessons of development to a few key items. But development is a comprehensive and multi-faceted process that transcends simplification to any single recipe. Accordingly, without trying to imply a hierarchy of importance, the most important lessons we have learned from reviewing the experience of four decades of development assistance can be grouped under the following headings:

The Proper Unit of Assessment: The Country

Although global trends and resource endowment are extremely important, the key development decisions are made primarily at the country level. Let us take, for example, two Asian countries, both allied with the United States, both adopting liberal economic policies, both having a large U.S. military presence, both receiving significant U.S. aid, both having had dictatorships with varying degrees of corruption—the Philippines and Korea. Thirty years ago the Philippines had three times the per capita income of Korea. Today, Korea has more than three times the per capita income of the Philippines.

In reviewing the evidence for sixty developing countries over twenty-three years, the World Bank found that those countries that focused on human resource development *and* had a sound macroeconomic management experienced an annual GDP growth rate that was a whopping 2.5 percent *higher* than those that did neither (figure 3-1).

It is interesting to note (figure 3-1) that if two countries' GDP were 100 at the start of the period and one followed sound macro-management policies *and* focused on human resource development, that country would achieve an annual growth rate of 5.5 percent. If the other did neither, it would achieve about 3 percent growth per year. At the end of the 23 years, their GDPs would stand at 342 and 197 respectively, a difference of 145, a *difference* almost one-and-a-half times the total GDP of 23 years earlier.

Figure 3-1 also shows that if a country performed well on only *one* of the two key indicators, it would achieve an increment of 0.8 percent over a country that followed neither, but good performance on both would generate significant synergies and yield an increment of 2.5 percent, not just of 1.6 percent.

Recognizing that the country is the critical unit of decisionmaking in today's world and that national policies are crucial to everything occurring in a country does not mean that there should not be major efforts at promoting regional cooperation and, ultimately, integration. Farsighted policies must take account of regional realities and promote the welfare of others as well as that of the country concerned.

Figure 3-1. Policy Distortion, Education, and Growth in GDP, Sixty Developing Countries, 1965–87

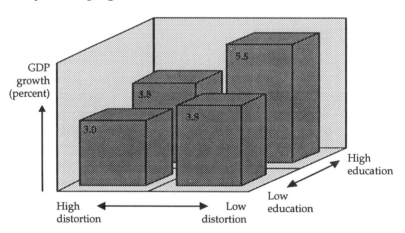

Note: High distortion reflects a foreign exchange premium of more than 30 percent; low distortion, a premium of 30 percent or less. Education is measured by the average years of schooling, excluding postsecondary schooling, of the population aged fifteen to sixty-four. High education is defined here as more than 3.5 years; low education, 3.5 years or less.

Source: World Bank, *World Development Report 1991: The Challenge of Development* (New York: Oxford University Press, 1991), 5.

Human Resource Development

Today the central importance of human resource development (HRD) is universally agreed. In a series of important reports UNDP has highlighted "human development" as a central concept and has done some very interesting work to measure a Human Development Index (HDI).[37]

Ultimately, however, the reasons why some countries are caught in the vicious circle of continuing poverty and low HRD tend to be institutional, governmental, and political.

Box 3-1. Ghana: Education Sector Adjustment Promotes Equity

A series of recent operations have supported Ghana's continuing education reform program.[1] Adjustment measures have been applied under the program, including a reduction in the proportion of secondary and tertiary boarding students; creation of a bulk purchasing system to lower student feeding costs; reductions in nonteaching staff; a freeze in the number of teaching posts; fee increases to help cover the costs of food, exercise books, and texts; and introduction of a loan scheme at the university level. The government also is attempting to rationalize the university system by establishing staffing norms, increasing student-teacher ratios, and consolidating nonviable programs and departments. The savings realized through the adjustment program have contributed to a substantial increase in basic education enrollments, improved allocation of financial resources, curriculum development, broad-based training of education staff, development and supply of instructional materials, and strengthened supervision. The ultimate goal of the three credits is a more cost-effective and equitable education system.

1. World Bank, "Report and Recommendation of the President of the International Development Association to the Executive Directors on a Proposed Credit of SDR 28.5 Million to the Republic of Ghana for an Education Sector Adjustment Credit," Report P-4311-GH (Washington, D.C., November 13, 1986); and World Bank, "Second Education Sector Adjustment Credit—Ghana," Report P-5244-GH (Population and Human Resources Operations Division, Western Africa Department, Washington, D.C., April 1990); and internal World Bank report, 1991. *Source:* World Bank, *Poverty Reduction Handbook* (Washington, D.C., 1993), 7-18.

Some projects have addressed these issues (box 3-1), but they are frequently stymied by the absence of the proper macroeconomic environment.

The Importance of the Macro Framework

The lessons of country performance among developing countries show that sound macro policies have much to do with performance. Evidence gathered by the World Bank by recalculating ex post facto the rates of return on 1,200 projects in 60 developing countries over 21 years (1968 to 1989) shows that in every kind of investment, public or private, in every sector, the rate of return increases as macroeconomic management improves (table 3-1). In this analysis the four

Table 3-1. Economic Policies and Average Economic Rates of Return for Projects Financed by the World Bank and the IFC, 1968–89

Policy distortion index	All projects	All public projects	Public agricultural projects	Public industrial projects	Public projects in nontradable sectors	All private projects
Trade restrictiveness						
High	13.2	13.6	12.1	INSF	14.6	9.5
Moderate	15.0	15.4	15.4	INSF	16.0	10.7
Low	19.0	19.3	14.3	INSF	24.3	17.1
Foreign exchange premium						
High (200 or more)	8.2	7.2	3.2	INSF	11.5	INSF
Moderate (20–200)	14.4	14.9	11.9	13.7	17.2	10.3
Low (less than 20)	17.7	18.0	16.6	16.6	19.3	15.2
Real interest rate						
Negative	15.0	15.4	12.7	12.7	17.9	11.0
Positive	17.3	17.5	17.0	17.8	17.9	15.6
Fiscal deficit[a]						
High (8 or more)	13.4	13.7	11.7	10.3	16.6	10.7
Moderate (4–8)	14.8	15.1	12.2	21.0	16.8	12.2
Low (less than 4)	17.8	18.1	18.6	14.1	18.2	14.3

Note: INSF, insufficient number of observations (fewer than ten) to make inferences.
a. Percentage of GNP.
Source: World Bank, *World Development Report 1991: The Challenge of Development* (New York: Oxford University Press), 82.

major macroeconomic management indicators taken were the trade regime, the exchange rate, interest rates, and the deficit.

The importance of sound macro-management should also go beyond the fiscal balances to ensure proper use of funds being expended. Transparency in understanding who pays and who benefits is essential to establish credible policies on such issues as subsidies (see box 3-2).

The Need for a Poverty-Focused Growth Strategy

Although it is recognized that growth is "a necessary but not sufficient condition" for development and that poverty reduction is a sine qua non for a successful development strategy, some still doubt the importance of directly tackling poverty and empowering the vulnerable.[38] Much as the "trickle-down" theorists of the 1950s used to say, they argue that growth by itself is enough. This is misconceived. *World Development Report 1990* provides a clear statement that it is difficult to sustain high growth rates if the social dimensions of development are not taken into account. *Human Development Report 1990* forcefully made the case for focusing on the social (human) as well as the economic aspects of development.

That growth is necessary but not sufficient for development can best be shown through the graph in figure 3-2. The graph plots the annual GDP growth rates, with the annual percentage reduction in head count index for thirteen developing countries. Although the time period and length of time are not necessarily the same for all countries, this does not affect the stylized facts obtained from the graph.

From the graph it is possible to see the correlation between growth rates and the annual reduction in poverty. Economies with high growth rates, such as Costa Rica, Indonesia, Malaysia, Singapore, and Taiwan(China) managed to achieve very significant reductions in poverty. Put another way, economies with lower growth rates have not had notable success in reducing poverty.

The case of Sri Lanka is instructive. Sri Lanka (along with China) is notable for having achieved levels of welfare (measured by infant mortality, life expectancy, and other indicators) far ahead of most

Box 3-2. Subsidies: Who Pays and Who Benefits?

Subsidies have always been one of the most favored means for governments to address the needs of the poor, but a series of studies in several African countries shows that in many cases subsidies have not worked. The benefits were "hijacked" by the middle class and the lower middle class, especially in urban areas. Meanwhile, the burden of financing the cost of the programs has shifted to the really poor, especially the farmers. This pernicious situation, in which the poor are financing benefits for the less poor, is frequently being defended by well-meaning academics and politicians in the name of protecting the interests of the poor themselves.

Exploding this myth is what makes these recent studies so important. Take the case of Côte d'Ivoire's Housing Agency in 1985 (much has changed since then, but the facts of that case are instructive):

First: Like many West African countries, the primary source of government revenue in Côte d'Ivoire was direct and indirect taxation of export crops (cocoa, coffee) produced largely by poor smallholder farmers.

Second: The government funded many urban subsidy programs, such as public housing. One public housing agency managed some 17,000 units. Low rents were supplemented by a transfer from the budget, whose main revenue source was the difference between the cocoa and coffee prices paid to the farmers and the world market price obtained by the government.

Third: A detailed survey showed that 86 percent of those living in these 17,000 units were above the poverty line. The remaining 14 percent were very close to the poverty line. The bulk of the smallholder farmers were below the poverty line.

To the credit of the country's leaders, when confronted by these facts, they acted. While raising rents was not politically feasible, the units were sold to the tenants. All the tenants were able to buy the units, and the 17,000 units were sold in six months. The reality of Côte d'Ivoire's public housing is not unique. In many, if not most, other countries the benefits are not going to the poorest citizens, as intended by the designers of the subsidy programs. Côte d'Ivoire, however, was unique in having the statistical data to document the case and in having a political leadership willing to act on these findings.

In Ghana the share of revenue by sector going to poor households is 24 percent for cocoa, 38 percent for oil palm, 35 percent for groundnut, 36 percent for yam/cocoyam, and 26 percent for maize.[1] Thus, at the margin, every cedi used in raising the producer price of cocoa will be divided in the ratio of 1 to 3.2 between poor and nonpoor households. The ratio for maize is 1 to 2.8, for oil palm 1 to 1.6, for groundnut 1 to 1.9, and for yam/cocoyam 1 to 1.8. The poverty profile shows a much higher subsidy efficiency ratio for the latter three crops. Therefore, poverty-sensitive price policy should concentrate on oil palm, groundnut, and yam/cocoyam for price increases, on cocoa and maize for price decreases.

In Côte d'Ivoire, as in Ghana, less than one-third of total rice sales is accounted for by poor households.[2] However, while the poor contribute only 9 percent to total rice consumption, their share in total food consumption is 13 percent. If the choice for agricultural price policy is reducing the producer price or increasing the consumer price, the poverty profile suggests that increasing the consumer price will do least damage to the poor at the aggregate national level. Similarly, if the choice is between increasing the producer price or reducing the consumer price, the former has priority in a poverty-focused strategy.

Today, in an increasing number of West African countries similar studies are yielding valuable insights into the questions of government expenditures, subsidy policies, and who the real beneficiaries are. In Ghana the "Poverty Profile" made it possible to assess a whole range of price options on different commodities and to show that there may be different ways of spending the same money on different goods and services to increase the benefits to the poor.

Is it not time that all thinking people should transcend rhetoric in discussing subsidies? Should we not be looking beyond the slogans to ask who pays and who benefits?

1. E. Oti Boateng and others, *A Poverty Profile for Ghana 1987–88*, SDA Working Paper 5 (Washington, D.C.: World Bank, 1990).
2. Ravi Kanbur, *Poverty and the Social Dimensions of Structural Adjustment in Côte d'Ivoire*, SDA Working Paper 2 (Washington, D.C.: World Bank, 1990).
Source: Ismail Serageldin, "Subsidies: Who Pays and Who Benefits?" *Al-Ahram* (November 14, 1991): 4.

other countries at the same level of per capita income. But because
Sri Lanka did not pursue adequate pro-growth policies, it has had
limited success in the speed with which it could reduce the number
of people living in poverty, as measured by the number of persons
or households living at incomes below a national poverty line. In
other words, a country can go only so far in redistributing the available resources; it must also increase the size of the available
resources. Thus, Sri Lanka is shown in the graph as having had low
growth rates combined with low poverty reduction levels. This
points to the often confusing difference between reduction of
inequality and reduction of *poverty*.

Furthermore, there is ample evidence that redistribution itself is
much more difficult without growth. Elites are more protective of
their share of a fixed or stagnating pie. In a situation of rapid growth
it is easier to direct a disproportionately larger share of the incre-

Figure 3-2. GDP Growth and Incidence of Poverty Trends

Annual percentage reduction in headcount index

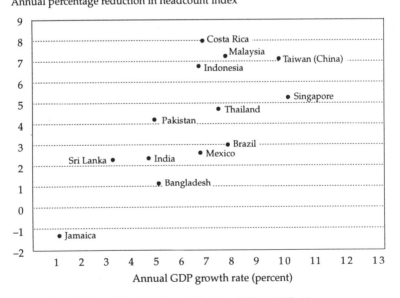

Source: Ismail Serageldin, *Development Partners* (SIDA, 1993), 48.

ment toward the more disadvantaged groups, thereby simultaneously achieving the reduction of poverty, more equitable distribution, and the rapid expansion of the available resources and options.
Finally, it is also important to note that no real transformation of an
economic base is likely to occur in a context of stagnation.

Indeed, the graph is very compelling in showing the remarkable performance of Taiwan (China) and Singapore, economies that are not
usually thought of as aggressively pursuing anti-poverty programs.
The very rapid growth rates of their economies provided sufficiently
large increments to allow them to deal quite effectively with poverty
reduction while pursuing the transformation of their productive base.

Yet, the reading of the graph as a simple relation between growth
and poverty reduction is only one side of the story. It is far more
interesting to focus on the *differences* in country experiences that it
brings out (see figure 3-3). A vertical line drawn at the 7 percent

Figure 3-3. GDP Growth and Incidence of Poverty—Differences

Annual percentage reduction in headcount index

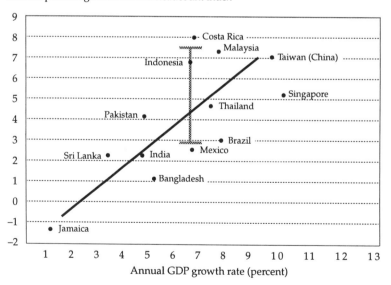

Source: Ismail Serageldin, *Development Partners* (SIDA, 1993), 49.

growth rate shows many countries with the *same* (or similar) growth rates but with vastly different rates of success in poverty reduction. Costa Rica, Malaysia, and Indonesia, with approximately the same growth rates as Brazil and Mexico, were able to reduce poverty close to three times the rate of Mexico and Brazil (7 to 8 percent versus 2.5 to 3 percent). This points to the importance of combining an aggressive poverty reduction program with aggressive pro-growth policies in designing policy packages. Different policy choices will lead to vastly different effects on poverty, growth rates remaining the same.

It is not hard to conclude that what is urgently required is a combination of pro-growth *and* anti-poverty policies.

Hunger and Extreme Poverty

If a broad-based economic growth strategy is linked to an aggressive anti-poverty program, it will help reduce the incidence of poverty over time. Indonesia, for example, succeeded in reducing the proportion of the population living below the poverty line from 58 percent to 15 percent in one generation, despite the growth in population during that time. However, throughout the world, a significant number of people remain extremely poor and go hungry.

Close to 1.0 billion people still suffer from hunger and malnourishment in the world today. Over 1.1 billion people live on less than one dollar a day. Every day, 40,000 people die from hunger-related causes. Those who do not die outright are deprived of the most basic needs of human existence; their children are stunted in their growth and unable to realize the full potential of their genes.

From this perspective, hunger is surely the most abhorrent physical expression of absolute poverty for it is imprinted on human flesh and bones. Furthermore, it is not only the poor who are degraded by that condition; all of humanity is degraded by our tolerance for allowing one-sixth or more of the world's population to continue living, barely, in such conditions.

It is shameful for the nations of the world that have achieved so much in so many domains not to be taking the necessary actions to remove this blight from the face of the earth. It is all the more shameful because so much of the problem is avoidable. The abolition of hunger in our lifetime is a task to which all people of good conscience must rededicate themselves.

In the last century, some persons looked upon slavery and declared that it was unacceptable and unconscionable. They considered slavery degrading not only to the slaves but to those who tolerated its existence. They did not seek improvements in the living and working conditions of the slaves; they wanted to abolish slavery from the face of the earth. They were called the abolitionists.

I believe that, like slavery a century ago, hunger today is unconscionable and unacceptable. We must be the new abolitionists, those who, from every location and every forum, will do our utmost to address this challenge. We must do so, because it is a moral imperative.

Apart from the ethical issues, from an economic and political standpoint, we have no choice. It makes no sense to leave so many kindred souls living in misery and wretchedness, barely surviving, when they could be active contributors to the improvement of self and society.

Unfortunately wishing the problem away will not make it disappear. It will require the systematic application of sound economic policies, a sustained commitment to investment in human resources, and the promotion of policies that support the empowerment of the poor. It will require special attention to the needs of women, for the empowerment of women is at the core of any sustained action to deal with poverty and hunger. It will require sustained commitment and cooperation from the international community. It must be attacked with a broad-based poverty-reduction strategy, because it is extreme poverty, not insufficient food production, that is the cause of all hunger. After all, the United States, the world's most efficient producer of food on a massive scale, still has some people who go hungry.

Beyond this double-pronged attack of broad-based growth and investment in human resources based on sound macroeconomic policies, there is clearly a need to support direct intervention to improve food security and nutrition and reach the poorest. In recognition of these complementary aspects, the World Bank recently released a report, *The World Bank's Strategy for Reducing Poverty and Hunger: A Report to the Development Community*, which reaffirms these principles and brings together in one place the wide-ranging actions required to attack extreme poverty and hunger (box 3-3). It lists, among other things, the largely unknown expansion of Bank support for nutrition

---

Box 3-3. Actions to Reduce Hunger: The World Bank's Agenda

• Promote broad-based, employment-intensive growth and improved access of the poor to education, health care, and other social services by encouraging macroeconomic stability and openness of the trade regime, reducing direct and indirect taxation of labor and farm sectors, eliminating anti-employment taxes and credit subsidies, and accelerating redirection of social spending to education, health care, and other social services.

• Protect the poor and the hungry in structural and sectoral adjustment programs by increasing the income-earning potential and livelihood security of the poor, encouraging compensatory expenditures for vulnerable groups, improving targeting of food subsidies, and ensuring that funding for synergistic primary health, nutrition, and targeted food assistance programs remains sufficient.

• Promote greater beneficiary participation and decentralization of functions and fiscal resources to local governments and community groups by integrating the lessons from the learning groups on participation in the Bank's operations and by strengthening accountability of local leaders.

• Collaborate with other agencies in assisting borrowing countries to prepare and finance actions for implementing synergistic, low-cost, hunger-reducing health and nutrition interventions (including reducing vitamin A, iodine, and iron deficiencies) through dietary modification, expanded childhood immunization programs, and implementation of a program for the control of parasitic infections.

---

projects, which went from nearly $20 million five or six years ago to over $680 million last year. Many of these projects have improved people's lives. The Tamil Nadu Nutrition Project in India, for example, managed to reach 20,000 villages and 3 million children and significantly improved the nutritional level of 50 percent of those children.

In addition, the Bank has been exploring new ways of supporting complementary actions to reach the poorest of the poor. One initially promising avenue is to join with other donors to systematically provide support to micro-credit schemes that empower the poorest to pull themselves up by their bootstraps, such as the National Family Planning

---

• Encourage countries to shift to targeted food assistance programs that provide food entitlements to children, mothers, or entire families identified as being at risk of becoming malnourished or having low-birth-weight babies through programs of on site feeding, food stamps, or free ration cards, rather than take-home food distribution.

• Assist borrowing countries and implementing agencies in monetizing food aid and making funds available to finance food supplementation programs for nutrition education, micronutrient supplementation, and health.

• Provide prompt response to drought and famines by integrating the impact of drought into country assistance strategies, strengthening countries' capacities to prepare for drought and to mitigate its effects, assisting countries in designing strategies for stabilizing prices of staple foods in the event of large, temporary price shocks, and improving lending instruments to provide for greater flexibility.

• Evaluate and provide support for targeted income-generation programs in view of country-specific poverty strategies by improving education, facilitating informal sector activities, expanding micro-credit, providing special help for difficult agroclimate zones, and promoting land reform.

• Support agricultural research and extension to ensure long-term food supplies and improve rural incomes by emphasizing small farmer extension, strengthening national agricultural research systems, and mobilizing a continued high level of support for the Consultative Group on International Agricultural Research.

Coordination Board in Indonesia and the Grameen Bank in Bangladesh.

Undeniably, a sound, broad-based development strategy is required to have a significant effect on the reduction of poverty. This comprehensive strategy, however, must be supplemented by special attention to the needs of the ultra-poor, those who are truly hungry, whose condition is beneath any definition of human decency. It is not just a sensible economic and political and social policy; it is a moral imperative.

Environment and Sustainability

Awareness of the environment—its strengths and fragility—has added a new and critically important dimension to our view of development.

In much of the developed world, pollution, resource looting, and indifference to the future have given way to increasing environmental awareness. Increasingly, we are made aware of the global costs of past indifference, costs which may cumulatively trigger irreversible damage to our biosphere: the depleted ozone layer with its potential to significantly increase the incidence of skin cancer, or increasing carbon dioxide emissions and their potential to exacerbate global warming. The governments in the industrial countries are gradually building the legal and regulatory safeguards to protect what remains and—as far as possible—regain what has been damaged.

In many developing countries, however, this is not the case. Much of Sub-Saharan Africa, for example, suffers from extreme climatic conditions, eroding topsoil, diminishing tree cover, and changing patterns of wildlife movement, all of which bring severe and immediate problems for the rural population. Indeed, Sub-Saharan Africa is suffering from the intertwined nexus of problems relating to poverty, rapid population growth and environmental degradation (see box 3-4). It is an important reminder of the inseparable link between population and environment. Other regions (such as Brazil and South Asia) as well as Africa are losing the remaining rainforests and their irreplaceable biodiversity. But addressing many of these global problems puts the burden of the costs locally, while the

Box 3-4. The Population, Agriculture, and Environment Nexus in Sub-Saharan Africa

Rapid population growth, environmental degradation, and slow agricultural growth in Sub-Saharan Africa are closely linked. Shifting cultivation and transhuman-pastoralism, adapted to low population density situations that were common in the Africa of the past, are environmentally damaging when population densities become high. With high population density, traditional farming and livestock practices cause soil and forest degradation. Soil degradation causes crop and livestock yields to decline, curtailing agricultural growth. Slow agricultural growth contributes to slow economic growth and inhibits the demographic transition to lower population fertility rates. A rapidly increasing population of poor rural people preys on the rural environment, wildlife, forests, and land for survival.

Traditional approaches, which emphasized supplying services and technologies, must be complemented by a strategy of promoting demand for (1) appropriate agricultural practices and inputs, (2) fewer children, and (3) conservation of resources.

• Demand can be promoted by removing policy that distorts prices and incentives away from intensive agricultural production. Only intensification of production can accommodate expanded agricultural output with natural resource conservation. Farmers must be the actors, and for this they require incentives.

• More emphasis is required on "sustainable" agriculture involving agroforestry, contour farming on slopes, and the use of mulch and natural or organic fertilizer (animal manure). Integration of crop and livestock on the same farms, including using animal power where appropriate, and soil conservation techniques such as terracing, the use of grasses, intercropping, and tree farming will all be important. Agricultural research and extension should focus much more on these types of technologies, and proportionately less on crop variety improvement and use of chemical inputs and farm mechanization. Women must become the focus of such efforts.

• The main environmental policies needed are establishment and maintenance of conservation areas, taxation and regulation of logging, and community participation in management of delicate areas in which local communities derive benefits as well as maintain responsibilities.

(Box continued on the following page.)

benefits accrue globally. Hence, a special assistance mechanism was required. This was the *raison d'être* for the Global Environment Facility (GEF) (box 3-5).

The nineteenth-century model of unfettered expansion often

Box 3-4 (continued)

However, successful agricultural intensification that induces rural people to settle, combined with much slower population growth, are the critical elements for slowing degradation of the rural environment.
  • These conservation and agricultural practices can be joined in land use plans, which will be important for promoting intensification of farming; protect valuable natural ecosystems; and defining areas for forestry exploitation, water resource management, and pasture management.
  • To encourage investment and conservation, resource ownership and land tenure need to be clarified, giving legal recognition to traditional common-property management and private ownership and reducing state ownership.
  • The most important instruments for promoting demand for smaller families will be expansion of educational programs for girls and employment opportunities for women and improvment of information on health and nutrition, in all cases through the use of community groups, NGOs, and the private sector. This will be necessary if the supply-side measures of family planning are to work.
  • Investing in and maintaining rural infrastructure, especially roads, water supply, and sanitation, are needed to improve production incentives, agricultural productivity, and health.
These findings are supported by the experiences of Botswana, Kenya, Mauritius, and Zimbabwe, countries in which total (population) fertility rates are declining. These countries have a relatively dense population on cultivable land, relatively high female education rates, relatively low infant mortality, active family planning programs, among the best performing agricultural sectors, and relatively good food security situations. Some success is being obtained with natural resource management as well.

Source: Kevin Cleaver and Götz A. Schreiber, *Reversing the Spiral: The Population, Agriculture, and Environment Nexus in Sub-Saharan Africa,* (Washington, D.C.: World Bank, 1994)

Box 3-5. The Global Environment Facility

The Global Environment Facility (GEF) has been transformed from a short-term experimental program into a permanent financial mechanism that will provide grants and concessional funds to developing countries for projects and other activities that protect the global environment.

The GEF covers four global environmental problems: climate change, the destruction of biodiversity, the pollution of international waters, and ozone depletion. The problem of land degradation, in the form of desertification and deforestation, is also part of the GEF's remit insofar as it relates to one or more of the main focal areas. GEF resources are available only to cover the difference between the cost of a project in one of the four focal areas that is undertaken with global environmental objectives in mind, and the cost of an alternative project that the country would have implemented in the absence of global environmental concerns.

The governance arrangements adopted for the new GEF contain elements of both the United Nations and Bretton Woods institutional models. They include a universal assembly that will meet every three years to review the facility's policies. The Council, which constitutes the main governing body of the new GEF, will meet at least twice a year. It will consist of 32 members representing 16 developing countries, 14 industrial countries, and 2 countries with economies in transition.

Responsibility for the conduct of the Council's business will be shared between an elected chairperson (as is the practice in the UN) and the GEF's chief executive officer (the Bretton Woods model). The CEO will also be the chairman of the GEF.

Decisions will be by consensus. When this is not possible, a vote may be taken. The GEF will have a "double majority" system requiring a 60 percent majority of all member countries as well as approval by donors representing at least 60 percent of contributions.

The GEF has been replenished with more than $2 billion for commitment over three years. This sum, which is about two and a half times larger than the pilot phase core fund that has been committed to over 100 projects, is in addition to resources channeled through regular official development assistance. The United States is the

(Box continued on the following page.)

became unrestricted exploitation. Plentiful labor and apparently unlimited natural resources seemed to justify a period of prodigal waste—of people, as well as of other "easily replaceable materials." Benevolent nature would provide; the mill owner lived a comfortable distance from the enterprise. Such a one-dimensional view was common. Indeed, the very few who thought differently— Robert Owen, for example—were derided as visionaries longing for utopia.

Much has been said about how pollution and development go hand in hand. This is not quite true. The situation varies. Different types of pollution tend to increase as per capita incomes grow. Others peak, then decline (see box 3-6). But these trends are not preordained. Conscious knowledge of these issues should lead to better policies to minimize the negative side effects of old patterns of

---

Box 3-5 (continued)

largest donor, having pledged SDR 307 million ($430 million). Japan will be the second largest donor, with some SDR 296 million, followed by Germany (SDR 171 million), France (SDR 102 million), and the United Kingdom (SDR 96 million). Nine developing countries have also announced pledges to the GEF.

The Geneva agreement to fund and restructure the GEF emphasizes the importance of leveraging additional resources from other sources, including the private sector; broadening the range of partners with access to GEF funds; and making more information available about the GEF and associated projects. It calls for GEF resources to be available for projects sponsored by the regional development banks, UN agencies, and national development agencies. Governments also stressed the important contribution that national and grassroots organizations can make to the GEF through project design and implementation.

The GEF is intended to be more than a channel for project financing. It should integrate the global environment into national development; encourage the transfer of environmentally sound technology and knowledge; and, crucially, strengthen the capacity of developing countries to play their full part in protecting the global environment.

Box 3-6. Economic Growth and the Environment— Friend or Foe?

Intuition suggests that economic growth causes environmental deterioration. Growth requires more raw material and energy inputs—causing depletion of natural resources. And growth brings more output, which causes more pollution. Fortunately, as in many other areas, facts give little support to intuition. Careful statistical analysis demonstrates three patterns of relationship between income growth and environmental damage. These are illustrated in box figure 3-6 (p. 44), which is derived from an analysis of cross-country data in the 1980s.

• *Some problems decline as income increases.* This happens because increasing income makes available the resources for society to provide public goods such as sanitation services and rural electricity, and once individuals no longer worry about day-to-day survival, they can devote resources to profitable investments in conservation. Polluted drinking water, lack of sewage facilities, indoor air pollution, and some types of soil erosion are examples of this type of relationship.

• *Some problems initially deteriorate but then improve as incomes rise.* Most forms of air and water pollution fit into this category, as do some types of deforestation and encroachment into natural habitats. This improvement is not automatic; it occurs only when countries deliberately introduce policies that allow increased income and technical progress to address environmental problems.

• *Some problems keep growing as income increases* (carbon and nitrogen oxide emissions and municipal wastes are examples). The costs of abatement are relatively high, while the costs of the damage are not yet perceived to be high—sometimes because they are borne by someone else. Once again, the key is policy. In most countries individuals and firms have little reason to reform until the right incentives are put into place.

Box figure 3-6 does not imply an inevitable relationship between income levels and particular problems. Individual countries can choose policies that result in much better (or worse) environmental conditions than those in other countries at similar income levels, and technological progress has enabled countries in recent decades to develop in a less damaging manner than was possible earlier.

Source: Andrew Steer, "The Environment for Development," *Finance & Development* 29 (2) (June 1992): 19.

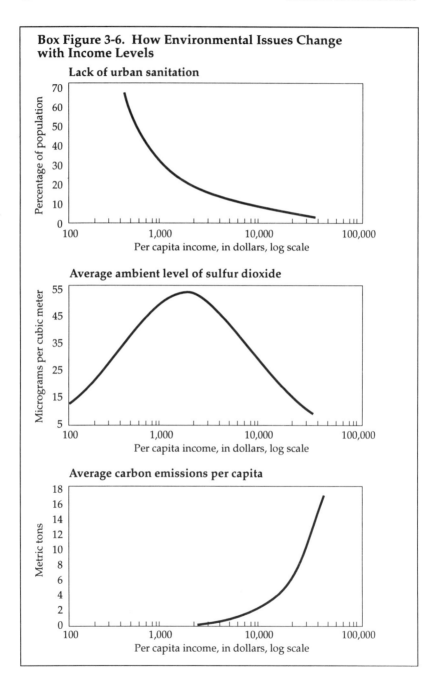

Box Figure 3-6. How Environmental Issues Change with Income Levels

development and to chart new paths that would embody environ-mentally sustainable development strategies from the start. In fact there is evidence that this is happening; yesterday's problems need not be repeated (see figure 3-4).

There is evidence that pollution is reversible. The rich countries have been able to make special efforts to regain lost ground and improve the environmental conditions for their citizens, especially in terms of urban pollution (see box 3-7). Thus, the poor tend to suf-fer most from environmental degradation. Figure 3-5 shows how soot and smoke are worsening in poor countries and improving in middle- and high-income countries.

This disparity need not be so. Not only can development be envi-ronmentally responsible, but past mistakes can also be reversed. Rivers can be reclaimed, woods can be restored. The environment is not only the scene against which development must unfold—it is an essential dimension of development. Resources used to improve water quality can, for example, be more than regained by the result-ing lower incidence of water-borne diseases and consequent lower

Figure 3-4. Yesterday's Problems Need Not Be Repeated

How technological change and environmental awareness have resulted in reduced soot and smoke emissions in the last two decades

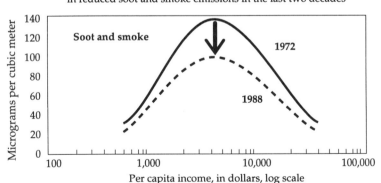

Note: Figure is based on cross-country regressions for the 1972–88 period. Per capita incomes are in 1985 purchasing power parity terms.
Source: Andrew Steer, "The Environment for Development," *Finance & Develop-ment* 29 (June 1992): 19.

Box 3-7. The Poor Suffer Most from Environmental Damage

Environmental damage can hurt people in three ways: it can harm their health; it can reduce their productivity and income; and it can spoil their quality of life for aesthetic, recreational, and spiritual reasons. The poor suffer disproportionately, particularly from health and productivity impacts.

• It is the poor who suffer from water contamination and lack of sanitation. For the most part, it is the poorest 1.7 billion people in the world who suffer from unsanitary conditions and the poorest 1 billion who have no access to piped water. The 2 million infants who die each year from such conditions are almost all from poor families. Ensuring sanitation and clean water for all—perhaps the greatest environmental challenge of the coming generation—would profoundly reduce poverty and human misery. In addition to preventing these 2 million deaths, it would result in 200 million fewer episodes of diarrheal illnesses annually, 300 million fewer cases of roundworm, 150 million fewer cases of schistosomiasis, and 2 million fewer cases of guinea worm.

• It is mainly the very poor who cook on open stoves using fuelwood, dung, and other biomass fuels. An estimated half billion women and children suffer severe health threats from such conditions. Recent studies in Nepal and India of nonsmoking women who are exposed to biomass smoke have found extraordinary levels of respiratory disease and premature death compared to male heavy smokers. Lack of affordable alternative energy sources is the cause. Improved stoves and public health education can play an important role, but the solution to this devastating environmental problem will be found only in rising incomes and increased access to modern energy sources.

• It is mainly very poor farmers who suffer depletion of their soils, not because they are producing too much but because they lack the financial resources (and sometimes the technical knowledge) to invest in soil conservation and fertilization. Similarly, it is the poorest farmers, denied legal tenure to land or access to extension and credit services, who, due to large family size and declining incomes, are forced to reduce fallow periods and to move onto marginally productive land and hillsides.

In each of these cases policies for development and policies for sound environmental stewardship are identical. Rising incomes and better access to publicly provided services (sanitation, education, extension, credit) are absolutely essential for a sustainable future.

Note: For further discussion see World Bank, *World Development Report 1992: Development and the Environment* (New York: Oxford University Press, 1992).

health care costs. Programs for reducing air pollution, reversing deforestation, and disposing of waste will produce, along with lesser financial benefits for polluters, fewer premature deaths, less frequent flooding, and lower rates of disease, respectively.

Environmental neglect has all too concrete consequences for productivity, income, and level of living. Declining fisheries, polluted groundwater, silting of ports, rivers, and reservoirs, and acid rain carry unacceptably high price tags. These are deplorable in developed

Figure 3-5. Urban Air Pollution: Average Concentrations of Suspended Particulate Matter, by Country Income Group

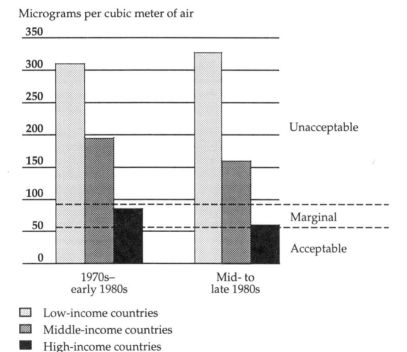

Micrograms per cubic meter of air

Low-income countries
Middle-income countries
High-income countries

Note: Periods of time series differ by site. World Health Organization guidelines for air quality are used as the criteria for acceptability.
Source: World Bank, *World Development Report 1992: Development and the Environment* (New York: Oxford University Press, 1992), 5.

countries; they are intolerable in many parts of the developing world.

In short, investment in development without equal attention to the environment precludes sustainability. The inevitable accumulating costs of neglect will eventually drain the benefits expected from development-centered initiatives. That both concerns can be integrated into a coherent general approach is the theme of the World Bank's

---

Box 3-8. The Earth Summit Accords, 1992

• *The Rio Declaration on Environment and Development*, emanating from the "Earth Summit," The UN Conference on Environment and Development (UNCED) in Rio de Janeiro in July 1992, states twenty-seven basic principles to guide national and international policies. It acknowledges that poor countries have a "right to development" and that rich countries bear a special responsibility "in view of the pressures their societies place on the global environment." The principles cover the link between environment and development, the sovereign right of states to exploit their own resources (without damage to others), international cooperation in eradicating poverty, women's role in sustainable development, and the use of economic instruments in environmental and development policy.

• *Agenda 21*, UNCED's blueprint for environmental action, aims at integrating environment and development. It addresses more than 100 program areas, including climate change, marine pollution, deforestation, desertification, human resources, and sustainable agriculture. It will be supported by new financial resources, improved access to environmentally sound technologies, and strengthened institutional capacity in developing countries. States were called on to prepare sustainable development plans outlining their environmental problems, strategies, programs, and priorities for implementing Agenda 21. Support for these programs should use the gamut of existing funding mechanisms.

Agenda 21 also calls for innovative financing to generate new public and private flows through greater use of debt swaps, economic and fiscal incentives, and reallocation of military resources to development. Existing aid consortia, consultative groups, and roundtables were asked to support these country-based programs by integrating environmental and development assistance strategies and by adjusting their membership and operations. UNCED requested the UN General Assembly at its September 1992 session to establish an intergovernmental committee to negotiate an international convention to

World Development Report 1992, presented at the United Nations Conference on Environment and Development (UNCED) in Rio.[39]

UNCED itself marked an important global milestone in which the case for "environmentally sustainable development" was universally recognized. A bold agenda for the future was drafted, and important accords were executed (box 3-8).

---

combat desertification, particularly in Africa. A Sustainable Development Commission will be established under ECOSOC to coordinate UNCED results.

• The *Climate Change Convention,* signed by 155 countries, aims at stabilizing concentrations of greenhouse gases to retard global warming. The agreement contains general commitments for all parties but specifies no targets or timetables for emission reductions. Industrial countries are required to adopt policies to limit emissions and "sources" of greenhouse gases and enhance carbon-absorbing "sinks" such as forests. Developing countries' obligations to implement their commitments depend on the financial resources and technology available beyond their overriding priorities of economic and social development and poverty reduction. This convention became effective on March 21, 1994.

• The *Convention on Biodiversity,* signed by 157 countries, aims to protect and sustain the earth's living resources and ecosystems and to share the benefits of genetic resources. Parties to it are required to identify important areas of biological diversity, conserve diversity at the site of origin and elsewhere, regulate access to genetic resources, and transfer technology relevant to the conservation and sustainable use of biological diversity on mutually agreed terms. Industrial countries are called upon to provide financial and technical resources to share equitably with developing countries the results of biotechnological research and development originating on their soil. This convention became effective on December 29, 1993.

• The *Principles for a Global Consensus on Forests* aim to reconcile potential conflicts among the objectives of sound management, conservation, and development of forests. The principles take into account the many functions of forests, including traditional uses, as well as the potential for their development through sustainable forest management.

Source: World Bank, *World Bank and the Environment 1992* (Washington, D.C. 1992), 9–10.

Women's Education and the Role of Women

That the role of women in development is essential is now widely accepted.[40] Yet, even though the benefits of such actions are no longer contested, obstacles to the empowerment of women persist. The obstacles lie in the male-dominated sociopolitical culture. This cultural bias, which results in abnormal infant and child mortality rates for females in many parts of the developing world,[41] is graphically described in box 3-9.

The key is female education. Without question, the single most effective way to empower women and to reap the social benefits of that empowerment is through education. In a recent essay Lawrence Summers provides some vivid statistics. The best available estimates suggest that each year of additional schooling of women reduces under-five child mortality by 10 percent[42] and reduces female fertility by approximately 5 to 10 percent.[43] The costs of improving the educational status of girls are minimal. Indeed:

> Raising the female primary school enrollment rate of girls to equal the male primary school enrollment rate in the world's low-income countries would involve educating an additional 25 million girls each year at a total cost of approximately $938 million . . . Raising the secondary school enrollment of girls to equal the secondary school enrollment rate of boys would involve educating an additional 21 million girls at a total cost of $1.4 billion. Eliminating educational discrimination in the low-income parts of the world would thus cost a total of $2.4 billion. This represents less than one-quarter of one percent of their GDP, less than two percent of their government consumption spending, less than one percent of their investment in new capital goods, and less than 1/10 of their defense spending.[44]

The immediacy of the payoff from increased female education in terms of reduction in infant mortality is captured in figure 3-6,

Box 3-9. One Hundred Million Women Lost?

The male/female ratios of the population are largely the result of biological determinants. In the OECD countries women comprise slightly more than 51 percent of the population. In Latin America and Sub-Saharan Africa the ratios range from slightly under 51 percent to slightly less than 49.5 percent. But in Asia the figures are dramatic: women represent 48.5 percent of the population in China, 48.1 percent in India, and 47.6 percent in Pakistan—the lowest share in the developing world.[1]

This discrepancy lies behind a stunning conclusion, first advanced by Amartya K. Sen, namely that 100 million women are missing. Sen rightly claims that this is "one of the more momentous problems facing the contemporary world."[2] The magnitude of the problem has been confirmed by Ansley Coale, who used slightly different assumptions but arrived at an estimate of 60 million missing women—still a staggering figure, which as he says "confirmed the enormity of the problem."[3]

The explanations for the missing women are, fundamentally, higher death rates for young girls in societies that discriminate against women through neglect and reduced opportunities for girls. In some cases selective abortion of female fetuses has been reported,[4] but it is undoubtedly higher mortality rates at ages one to four that account for the bulk of the discrepancies.

Beyond the moral outrage that such findings rightly generate, it is important to emphasize that they reflect societal attitudes inimical to development because empowering women through education and removing obstacles to their full participation in economic life demonstrably improves the developmental performance of any society.

Note: See also United Nations Development Programme, *Human Development Report 1991* (New York: Oxford University Press 1991), 27.

1. Lawrence H. Summers, *Investing in All the People*, EDI Seminar Paper (Washington, D.C.: World Bank, 1994), 2.

2. Amartya K. Sen, "Women's Survival as a Development Problem" (Comments prepared for the 1700th Stated Meeting of the American Academy of Arts and Sciences, March 8, 1989); and Sen, "More than 100 Million Women Are Missing," *New York Review of Books* 37 (December 20, 1990): 61–66.

3. Ansley Coale, "Excess Female Mortality and the Balance of the Sexes in the Population: An Estimate of the Number of 'Missing Females,' " *Population and Development Review* 17 (3) (September 1991): 517–23.

4. See Anouch Chahnazarian, "Determinants of the Sex Ratio at Birth (Hepatitis B)" (Ph.D. diss., Princeton University, Princeton, N.J., 1986).

Figure 3-6. Female Educational Attainment and Decline in Infant Mortality, Selected Economies, 1960–87

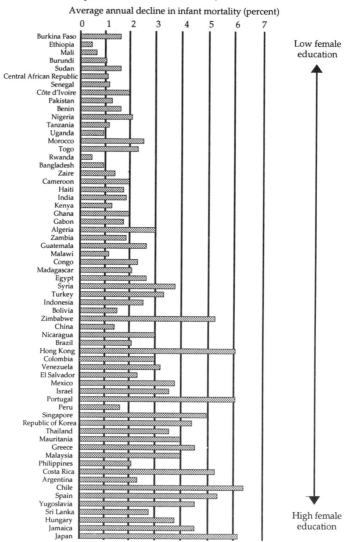

Note: Economies are listed in ascending order by level of female education, defined as the average years of schooling, excluding postsecondary schooling, of females age fifteen to sixty-four.
Source: World Bank, *World Development Report 1991: The Challenge of Development* (New York: Oxford University Press, 1991), 49.

which clearly shows very significant increases in the rate of annual reduction of infant mortality as women obtain more education.

In spite of this compelling evidence, the situation in many developing countries is sorely lacking. Sahelian Africa is probably the region most negatively affected (box 3-10).

The reasons for continuing low enrollments for girls are many and complex, and differ across levels of education and communities. For example, in communities in which girls marry young and become part of their husbands' families and in which sons are expected to sustain their parents as the latter age, parents perceive too few benefits from investing in their daughters' education. At the same time the actual cost of their daughters' education is often higher than their sons' because the time that girls spend in school is taken away from essential household chores. In other communities parents are more concerned with their daughters' safety and the propriety of the school environment than with the economic benefits or costs of the education. This concern is particularly pressing when schools are too far from home, lack appropriate sanitary facilities, and are staffed with male teachers. Finally, in many countries communities are simply unaware of the substantial benefits that educating girls offers to individuals and society.

Understanding these constraints on girls' school attendance has helped a number of countries design appropriate incentives to increase girls' enrollment. Some of the options:

• Morocco and Nigeria have launched information campaigns to encourage families to educate their daughters.

• Bangladesh, Morocco, and Pakistan have financed scholarships or stipends for girls to lower the cost of girls' education.

• China and India have changed their school schedules and calendars to accommodate girls' participation in the household economy.

• In Bangladesh and Pakistan, where safety concerns are foremost in parents' minds, lessening the distance from home to school, constructing closed latrines, establishing all-girl schools, and hiring female teachers have addressed important parental objections to girls' school attendance.

Box 3-10. Female Education in the Sahel

Despite the known benefits of increased female education, only 19 percent of women in the Sahel are literate, a rate lower than in any other world region. It is not surprising, then, that the Sahel also has the highest rates of fertility and child mortality, the lowest life expectancy, and the lowest girls' school enrollment rate of any other region. Consider the statistics:

• Individuals born in the Sahel can expect to live only 49 years, compared with a Sub-Saharan average of 53, and an average of 60 for all developing countries.

• In the Sahel 21 percent of the children die before the age of 5, a rate 30 percent higher than the average for Africa and double the average for all developing countries.

• Fertility rates among women in the Sahel average 6.4, a rate 25 percent higher than the average for developing countries.

• Only 35 percent of school-age girls and 52 percent of school-age boys are enrolled in primary school, compared with the Sub-Saharan averages of 72 and 82 percent, respectively. At the secondary level, only 8 percent of girls and 16 percent of boys are enrolled, compared with the Sub-Saharan averages of 17 and 23 percent.

If we accept even only part of the evidence that mothers' education is strongly linked to increased productivity, lower child mortality, and better family health and education, then, undoubtedly, sustained economic and social development will be slow in the Sahel unless educational opportunities are made more available to girls and women. It is within this context that all involved in education should place top priority on understanding the obstacles to female enrollment in educational programs and on designing effective measures to increase their participation.

Box Figure 3–10
Female Literacy in the Sahel Is the Lowest of Any Region . . .

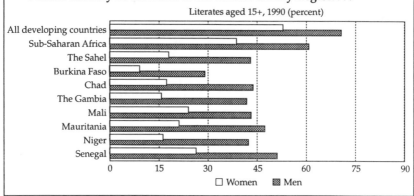

Literates aged 15+, 1990 (percent)

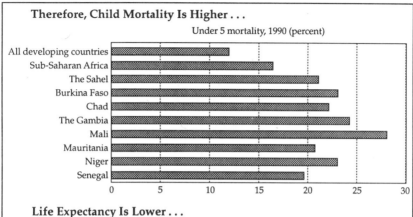

Therefore, Child Mortality Is Higher...

Under 5 mortality, 1990 (percent)

Life Expectancy Is Lower...

Life expectancy at birth, 1990 (years)

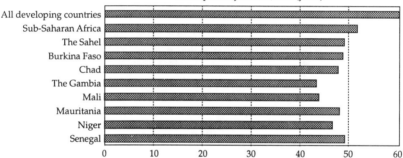

Fewer Girls Are Enrolled in School...

Children enrolled in primary school, 1990 (percent)

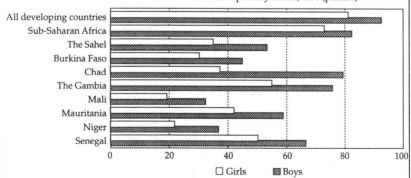

□ Girls ▒ Boys

... and the Cycle Continues in the Next Generation.

Source: "Promoting Girls' Education: A Key to Development in the Sahel" (World Bank, Sahelian Department, Population and Human Resources Division, Washington, D.C., September 1992).

Civil Liberties and the Role of Women

Where and how do women get more access to education? While
every society is different and has its unique specificities, it is interesting to note (figure 3-7) that the gender gap in women's access to education (measured as a ratio of female to male educational achieve-
ment in a country) is positively correlated with civil liberties. The
more civil liberties, the more likely that women will come closer to
men in terms of educational attainment. Figure 3-7 shows the positive relationship using the work of Gastil for the civil liberties

**Figure 3-7. Association between Political and Civil Liberties
and Women's Education, Selected Economies, 1973–86**

Ratio of female to male educational attainment

Note: Data are period averages for a sample of sixty-seven economies; data for 1974
were unavailable. Educational attainment is defined as the average years of
schooling, excluding postsecondary schooling, of the population aged fifteen to
sixty-four.
Source: World Bank, *World Development Report 1991: The Challenge of Development*
(New York: Oxford University Press, 1991), 50.

index.[45] Using the Humana index, the UNDP has similar findings.[46] This leads to a dual conclusion: first, that promoting female education is fundamental for reducing infant mortality, and second, that the promotion of civil liberties is likely to be helpful in this endeavor.

This is not an academic, long-term issue. It requires action *now*. The gender gap in today's educational enrollments will hobble developmental efforts twenty years from now. Figure 3-8 graphs the performance of various countries in 1985 at reducing infant mortality against the average level of educational attainment. As expected, the more educated a people, the lower their infant mortality rates. *But*, let us go back twenty years (to 1965), identify the countries that had a

Figure 3-8. The Effect of the Gender Gap in Education on Infant Mortality, 1985

Infant deaths per 1,000 live births, 1985

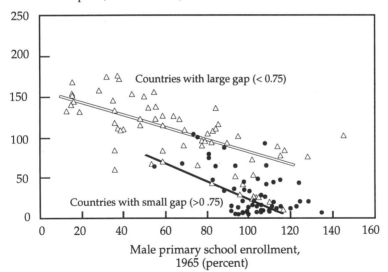

Male primary school enrollment,
1965 (percent)

Note: The figure assumes that primary school enrollment affects infant mortality twenty years later. The gender gap in education is the ratio of female to male enrollment at the primary school level. A large gender gap is an enrollment ratio for girls that is three-fourths or less that of boys.
Source: World Bank, *World Development Report 1991: The Challenge of Development* (New York: Oxford University Press, 1991).

large gender gap (less access to education for women), and plot a line on the 1985 graph for them alone. A large gender gap is defined by an enrollment ratio for girls that is three-fourths or less that of boys. If we then do the same for those with a small gender gap (more fairness to women in access to education), we find that while both lines slope downward (in other words, less infant mortality for more education), the low gender gap countries line is consistently below the other. The implication is that a fairer situation twenty years ago resulted in a significantly better performance today.

The situation is even more dramatic when we look at fertility decline as opposed to infant mortality. The analysis is the same, and

Figure 3-9. The Effect of the Gender Gap in Education on Total Fertility, 1985

Total fertility, 1985 (number of children)

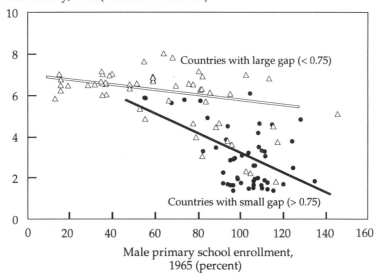

Male primary school enrollment,
1965 (percent)

Note: The figure assumes that primary school enrollment affects total fertility twenty years later. The gender gap in education is the ratio of female to male enrollment at the primary school level. A large gender gap is an enrollment ratio for girls that is three-fourths or less that of boys.
Source: World Bank, *World Development Report 1991: The Challenge of Development* (New York: Oxford University Press, 1991).

the lines in figure 3-9 are to be interpreted in the same way as those in figure 3-8. The low gender gap countries line is not only below the high gender gap countries line but has a considerably steeper slope.

All this highlights the absolute urgency to act now to address the needs of women today, lest we continue to pay the price of this neglect and inequity well into the future. Action to improve the status of women will be enhanced by efforts to increase civil liberties.

Governance and the Civil Society

The importance of good governance is now well acknowledged.[47] New international efforts against corruption (such as Transparency International)[48] are being added to well-established, long-standing efforts promoting human rights (such as Amnesty International).[49] What we are increasingly learning is that the promotion of good governance (as well as better socioeconomic performance) depends in large measure on the civil society.[50]

Traditional society is generally perceived as being dominated by family, clan, or ethnic loyalties. Those cross-cutting associations based on occupation or special interests that do exist play a minor role. As a modern state evolves, the network of associations becomes denser and civil society becomes more multidimensional. If democratic institutions are to emerge and endure, they must be anchored in a robust civil society. Thus part of the challenge of development is the nurturing of civil society.

Although political scientists have long recognized the crucial role of civil society in the development process, this dimension has been largely ignored by economists and has been generally absent from the programs of aid agencies. Institutional development has been conceived as a process of strengthening the role of public institutions. This has served to reinforce the dominance of the state and to weaken public accountability. What is needed is a systematic effort to combat this bias by assisting the growth of private sector institutions and nongovernmental organizations. This implies a recognition of the value of institutional pluralism and the need for a balance of power between the private and public domains and between central and local authorities.

The growth of civil society depends on respect for basic human rights. It means acceptance of:

- The freedom of association
- The freedom of information
- The rule of law.

Nurturing civil society is, therefore, an integral part of the pursuit of good governance. Indeed, a convincing case can be made that promoting the civic community is essential for nurturing good governance and effective, sustained socioeconomic development. The studies by Robert Putnam on Italy are most compelling (see box 3-11). It becomes clear that development assistance has a role to play in helping nurture the civil society.

With this end in view, aid agencies should fund specific initiatives in support of professional associations, chambers of commerce and industry, women's groups, local government, indigenous NGOs, and community organizations. This should be done to promote private sector and grassroots development as part of a strategy to strengthen civil society.

The Policy Framework

The best of present thinking indicates that a *human-centered, market-friendly approach* is the most effective approach to promoting development in a particular country. Such an approach is graphically presented in figure 3-10.

This approach focuses on human resource development, at the top, where the quality of a trained labor force can meet international standards of production and is able to receive the best and most up-to-date technology that the global economy has to offer. At the same time, at the domestic level of national enterprises functioning in the microeconomic context of the firm, such trained personnel command a premium wage and increase the returns to education (thereby reinforcing the motivation for education and training).

These same firms, in a sensibly managed economy with a stable macro framework that allows and encourages contact with the inter-

Box 3-11. A Convincing Case from Italy

In a landmark study presented in *Making Democracy Work: Civic Traditions in Modern Italy*, Robert D. Putnam of Harvard University and colleagues have made a convincing case that the existence of civic community is not only the precursor and guarantor of good governance but also the key to sustained socioeconomic development.

Strong civic community is defined as a preponderance of *voluntary horizontal associations,* in contrast to *hierarchical vertical associations,* and the *density* of these voluntary institutions, throughout the society. A matrix of voluntary horizontal associations is found in prosperous, rapidly developing northern Italy while the less developed, less effective south is characterized by autocratic vertical institutions.

But which is cause and which is effect? Does the north have a dense network of horizontal institutions (choral societies, soccer clubs, parent-teacher associations) because it is rich and can afford them? Or is it rich because it has good, responsive government nurtured by long-standing citizen involvement in many such voluntary horizontal institutions?

Putnam and his colleagues went back to data from the nineteenth century and the beginning of the twentieth century, when the socioeconomic structures and levels of development were similar in some northern provinces and some southern provinces but the horizontal and vertical slants of their civic associations were differentiated. They tested the hypotheses as to what best explained the observed socioeconomic structures and civic institutional structures of northern and southern Italy in 1970, when the Italian government abandoned its 100-year-old centralized administration and created twenty virtually identical regional governments, and what would best explain their disparate performance, twenty years later.

The results of their research are summarized by box figure 3–11 (p. 62), in which the thickness of the arrows indicates the strength of the relationships observed.

It seems clear that a strong, dense, horizontally structured civil society of voluntary associations is very likely to promote good governance and nurture sustained socioeconomic performance. Development partners would be well advised to nurture a strong voluntary civic community to promote sustained development over the long term.

(Box continued on the following page.)

national economy, are able to receive investments and capital from the global economy as they export goods and services. The links between the firms or productive units at the left of the diagram and the stable macroeconomy are tight and complex. They involve fiscal discipline and appropriate price and tax signals.

Finally, the macro-management of the economy must have close ties to the changing context of the global economy. It must be able to withstand shocks and continue to participate in the system of international trade and to attract capital for investments.

This general framework is just that: a framework. Strategies for each country must dictate the specific measures that are most appropriate for its circumstances. No single prescription will be generally applicable. What is suitable for Korea may not be applicable to Chad, and what is appropriate for Brazil has little to do with Senegal. But all developing countries would be well advised to

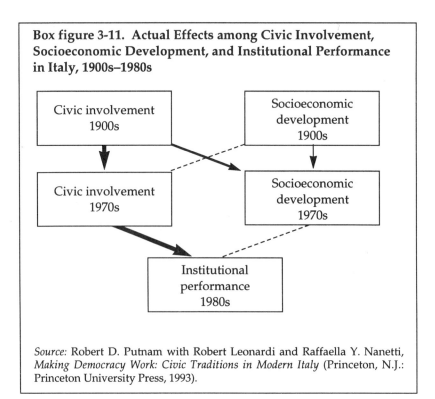

Box figure 3-11. Actual Effects among Civic Involvement, Socioeconomic Development, and Institutional Performance in Italy, 1900s–1980s

Source: Robert D. Putnam with Robert Leonardi and Raffaella Y. Nanetti, *Making Democracy Work: Civic Traditions in Modern Italy* (Princeton, N.J.: Princeton University Press, 1993).

invest in their human resources and to adopt a set of macro policies that would promote a stable (although dynamic) economic environment which is open to the world economy and provides an enabling environment in which each individual and each firm or productive unit can blossom to the maximum.

The Institutional Framework

Views about the most suitable institutional structures for development have varied over time, affected by the prevalent ideologies among donors and developing countries and by the emerging lessons of experience. Goran Hyden has captured in simplified diagrammatic terms the main points of this evolution over the last four

Figure 3-10. The Interactions in a Market-Friendly Strategy for Development

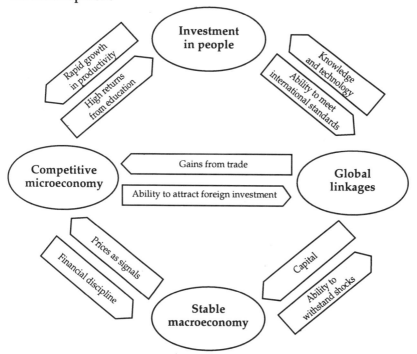

Source: World Bank, *World Development Report 1991: The Challenge of Development* (New York: Oxford University Press, 1991), 6.

decades. In reading the diagram (figure 3-11) one should remember
that the arrow does not come full circle to the starting point but
rather rises (into a third dimension) like a spiral, for we all learn from
past experience, donor agencies, and developing countries alike.

Fluctuating between an emphasis on management or participation
(horizontal axis) and the poles of growth and equity (vertical axis),
Hyden's "map" shows four quadrants, each of which represents a
dominant paradigm (identified near the intersect of the axes) and a
preferred institutional actor to promote development. Starting from
the upper left quadrant and going counterclockwise, we proceed
roughly along the decades from the late 1950s to the late 1980s.
Starting with "trickle-down" as a main concept and central government as the engine of development, we move past the late 1960s
toward "integrated development," especially for rural areas, managed by decentralized government administration.

This integrated approach dominated development projects of the
1970s. By the late 1970s, practitioners became disenchanted with

Figure 3-11. Shifts in the Development Paradigm

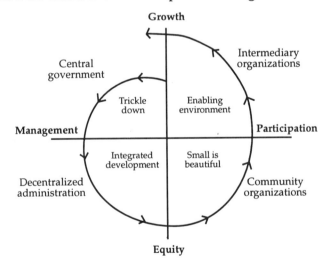

Source: Goran Hyden, "The Changing Context of Institutional Development in
Sub-Saharan Africa," in *Institutional and Sociopolitical Issues*, vol. 3 of *Background
Papers: The Long-Term Perspective Study of Sub-Saharan Africa* (Washington, D.C.:
World Bank, 1990), 44.

large bureaucracies and large projects as they gave more attention to local institutions and structures. The spirit of the times was captured by E. F. Schumacher's phrase, "Small is beautiful."[51] Community organizations and NGOs became important actors. They have contributed much to development and will continue to do so.[52] The fourth phase, starting in the 1980s, went beyond these micro approaches and sought systemic improvements by using intermediary organizations, mostly nongovernmental, to promote among other things the growth of local initiatives. The notion of an "enabling environment," a phrase coined by the Aga Khan at Nairobi, captures the spirit of this approach.[53] But, the main conclusion of this ongoing search is the recognition that institutional factors are essential in understanding how development works, and hence how to promote it most effectively.[54] Increasingly, development aid agencies are trying to promote both the systemic enabling framework *and* local capacity.[55] The Aga Khan Foundation's Rural Support Programme is one of the signal successes in this area (see box 3-12).

Privatization

The need to adjust the economic ownership structure in which the state dominated the economy has led to the need to "privatize" a number of state-owned enterprises (SOEs) in many countries. The experience with such efforts has been mixed, in that it has proved difficult to face the political and social costs of privatization, even when the need is clearly recognized, and to maintain a fully transparent process. But the evidence is overwhelming that ownership matters in promoting productivity. Figure 3-12 shows the productivity-ownership link in China, by province (1985–87).

But the decision on what to privatize will differ from country to country. In a recent survey of the lessons of experience, Kikeri, Nellis, and Shirley have provided a framework for decisionmaking (figure 3-13).[56] The financial returns from privatization can also be important (figure 3-14), but this is not always the case. Kikeri, Nellis, and Shirley observe:

Box 3-12. The Aga Khan Rural Support Programme, Pakistan

Over the last decade the situation has begun to change radically for the better in the high mountain valleys in the Northern Areas of Pakistan. The change has been wrought largely by the people themselves with help from the Aga Khan Foundation.

Per capita income for the area's 800,000 people was—and remains—way below Pakistan's average. Infrastructure was almost nonexistent. The people were scattered and unorganized. And as population pressures increased, there was no way of expanding the small family holdings without the construction of long irrigation channels to bring water down from the melting glaciers and streams. The downward economic spiral could be checked only if the people could work together to bring more land into cultivation.

A hybrid approach was forged that drew on the experience of collective agriculture in countries such as Japan and Bangladesh and on venture capitalism. In 1982 the Aga Khan Rural Support Programme (AKRSP) was launched. It identified the central factor in the region's decline as the power vacuum created when the fast-eroding feudal authority of the local chieftains was abolished by the central government in 1974.

"Our principal task is to build institutions, not run projects," says AKRSP Director Shoaib Sultan Khan. A representative organization was set up in each village to become the vehicle for the collective actions to enable villagers not just to survive but to reap the potential benefits of the opening in 1978 of the Karakoram Highway, which links the Northern Areas with the rest of Pakistan and China.

Staff from the Gilgit headquarters fanned out over the vast rugged region on foot, in jeeps, and by helicopter. They called the inhabitants together village by village and explained in a series of "dialogues" the terms of the proposed social contract. The program offers the incentive of a grant toward costs of an initial "productive physical infrastructure project" and technical advice from its team of experts. The funds purchase construction materials that cannot be found locally and pay a substantial part of wage costs. The villagers commit not only to carry out construction and maintenance but also to regular meetings and a collective savings program. As expected, the most popular infrastructure projects have been irrigation channels. Other projects include roads and protective dikes. Central to the strategy is that every project has an immediate impact on family income. At the same time it provides a new flow of income from which the villagers generate savings that become the collateral for future collective ventures. Village organization savings amount to 124 million rupees, and more than 10,000 villagers have been trained in social organization and technology. The program serves more than 2,000 village organizations, including more than 500 women's organizations.

AKRSP has been adopted as the model for rural support programs in the North-Western Frontier Province (NWFP) (Sarhad Rural Support Corporation) and Balochistan (Balochistan Rural Support Programme). It is also the model for the National Rural Support Programme (NRSP) of the government of Pakistan, for replication in 16 districts of Sindh, Punjab, the NWFP, and Baluchistan. AKRSP has attracted bilateral funding from ODA, the Commission of European Communities (CEC), the Canadian International Development Agency (CIDA), and the government of the Netherlands amounting to $40 million for the first half of the 1990s, plus a grant of $1 million from the World Bank for small enterprise development. AKRSP has also been contracted by the government of the Netherlands to help implement a $20 million water and sanitation program in the Northern Areas using village organizations. This project entails mediating relations between the government and villagers and helping government officials understand what villagers can do for themselves.

In its first evaluation report in 1987 the World Bank gave three main reasons for AKRSP's "impressive results": (1) the independence of the sponsoring agency from the government's bureaucracy, (2) the long-term nature of the program, which permits "the patient pursuit of much longer-term institutional and social objectives," and (3) bottom-up planning, in contrast to projects that offer a standard package of works and improvements on a take-it-or-leave-it basis.

The record so far is impressive, but, as the Bank's second evaluation in 1990 makes clear, so are AKRSP's challenges over the next ten years: adapting its model to be more demand-driven, establishing permanent successor institutions in the Northern Areas and Chitral, and reducing its dependence on donor funds and raising its level of self-sustainability.

Figure 3-12. The Productivity-Ownership Link in China, by Province, 1985–87

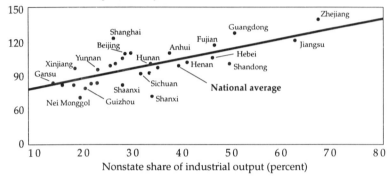

Index of total factor productivity

Note: Because of space limitations, only selected provinces are identified.
Source: Sunita Kikeri, John Nellis, and Mary Shirley, *Privatization: The Lessons of Experience* (Washington, D.C.: World Bank, 1992), 21.

Figure 3-13. Privatization: A Framework for Decisionmaking

Country conditions	Enterprise conditions	
	Competitive	*Noncompetitive*
High capacity to regulate; market-friendly	*Decision* • Sell	*Decision* • Ensure or install appropriate regulatory environment • Then consider sale
Low capacity to regulate; market-unfriendly	*Decision* • Sell, with attention to competitive conditions	*Decision* • Consider privatization of management arrangements • Install market-friendly policy framework • Install appropriate regulatory environment • Then consider sale

Source: Sunita Kikeri, John Nellis, and Mary Shirley, *Privatization: The Lessons of Experience* (Washington, D.C.: World Bank, 1992), 5.

Privatization revenues have been significant in some developing countries, particularly in Latin America, where large SOEs have been sold [figure 3-14]. But net revenues from SOE sales have usually been modest because most transactions have been small, the up-front costs associated with privatization (settlement of enterprise debt, unpaid taxes, and transaction fees) have been high, and sales have often been on installment plans. In Guinea, for example, total assets sold amounted to 21 billion Guinean francs, of which only 2 billion were paid (as of June 1991), as a result of lengthy repayment periods and defaults by purchasers. In Ghana only 57 percent of total sale proceeds has been paid to date.[57]

Ultimately, the lessons from the experiences with privatization are perhaps best captured by the checklist provided by Kikeri, Nellis, and Shirley (box 3-13).

The Need for a Public-Private Partnership

The discredited "statist" ideology should not be replaced by an equally sweeping confidence in the power of markets and the private sector

Figure 3-14. Gross Proceeds from Privatization, 1980–91
(millions of U.S.dollars)

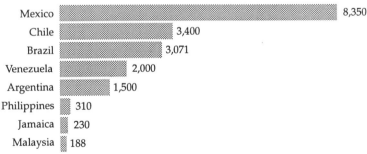

Note: Data are for 1980–91 except for Chile, 1973–91. Data include liquidations and any sale that reduces the government share in the firm to less than 50 percent; they exclude reprivatizations.
Source: Sunita Kikeri, John Nellis, and Mary Shirley, *Privatization: The Lessons of Experience* (Washington, D.C.: World Bank, 1992), 30.

Box 3-13. A Checklist for Privatization

• The more market-friendly a country's policy framework—and appropriate policy is correlated with capacity to regulate—the less difficulty it will have privatizing state-owned enterprises and the more likely the sale will turn out positively.

• State enterprises functioning in competitive markets, or in markets easily made competitive, are prime candidates for privatization. Compared with public monopolies, their sale is simple, and they require little or no regulation.

• An appropriate regulatory framework must be in place before monopolies are privatized. Failure to regulate properly can hurt consumers and reduce subsequent public support for privatization.

• Countries can benefit from privatizing management through management contracts, leases, contracting out, or concessions.

• The primary objective of privatization should be to increase efficiency—not to maximize revenue (for example, by selling into protected markets) or even to distribute ownership widely at the expense of managerial efficiency.

• Governments should experiment with "golden shares" and partial share offerings to win acceptance for foreign and other buyers, rather than restrict the market by excluding foreign investors and favoring certain ethnic groups.

• Avoid large new investments in privatization candidates: the risks usually outweigh the rewards. Rather, prepare for sale by carrying out legal, managerial, and organizational changes; financial workouts; and labor shedding.

• Experience shows that labor does not, and need not, lose in privatization if governments pay attention to easing the social cost of unemployment through adequate severance pay, unemployment benefits, retraining, and job-search assistance.

• Ideally, let the market set the price and sell for cash. Realistically, negotiated settlements and financing arrangements or debt-equity swaps may be unavoidable.

• In all privatizations in all countries, transactions must be transparent.

Source: Sunita Kikeri, John Nellis, and Mary Shirley, *Privatization: The Lessons of Experience* (Washington, D.C.: World Bank, 1992), 11.

alone to fulfill all the needs of society. The optimal balance is for the
state to limit itself to fundamental services that it must provide (such
as basic human resource development, infrastructure, and the creation and maintenance of an enabling environment) and leave to the
private sector the provision and distribution of most goods and services. This view of a mix of public and private investment is given
support by the World Bank's review of 650 projects in 60 developing
countries over the period 1968 to 1989 as shown in figure 3-15.

As shown in the graph, assuming reasonable macroeconomic poli-

**Figure 3-15. The Share of Public Investment in Total Investment
and the Rates of Return of Agricultural and Industrial Projects
Financed by the World Bank and the IFC, 1968–89**
(percent)

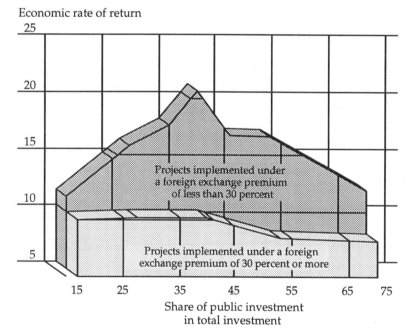

Note: Calculated for 650 public and private projects.
Source: World Bank, *World Development Report 1991: The Challenge of Development*
(New York: Oxford University Press, 1991), 86.

cies, it is not true that the less public investment, the better. In fact, a low share of public investment results in a lower rate of return, for the individual project (or investor) has to absorb the cost of producing the needed infrastructural support for the productive activity. As the public share in total investment rises, so does the rate of return. After a certain point, the public sector begins to "crowd out" the private sector in terms of access to credit and resources, and the rates of return decline again.

It is noteworthy, however, that if there is no sound macroeconomic management, exemplified in the graph by an exchange rate premium of more than 30 percent, then the whole effect is swamped by the macro distortion and the results are uniformly mediocre.

In addition, it is important to recognize the potential of the infor-

---

**Box 3-14. Microenterprises in Guinea-Bissau:
A Tool for Development**

One of the most successful Social Dimensions of Adjustment (SDA) programs has been in Guinea-Bissau. The Social Infrastructure Relief Project of about $20 million and its SDA component of about $1 million have been completed on time, and the IDA credit disbursed one year in advance. Analytical equipment was provided to the National Research Center, and studies were carried out on women in development, food security, microenterprises, and housing. A household survey (Priority Plus Survey) was carried out and final results disseminated. Hundreds of laid-off civil servants have been retrained through the Reorientation Unit and have taken new jobs.

The SDA in Guinea-Bissau wanted to address the problem of unemployment through microenterprises and the informal sector. Thus, the government requested a study financed through the SDA program to determine how to enhance development based on microenterprises. This study, which was aimed at understanding the composition of the informal sector in Bissau and at describing the processes that led to its development, was carried out in 1990 among 605 enterprises employing 2,129 people.

These enterprises belong to the service sector (43 percent), industry (30 percent), commerce (25 percent), and agriculture (2 percent). The typical profile of enterprises in Bissau's informal sector is individual enterprises (90 percent), of small scale (70 percent have fewer than 10

mal sector, both as a nursery of entrepreneurs and as the primary means of employment and self-employment for the poor (see box 3-14). The creation of an enabling environment to allow the private sector to flourish should also apply to the informal sector with its myriad microenterprises, with a view to assisting them to grow and enter the formal economy.

Debt and Foreign Direct Investment

The 1980s witnessed a severe and generalized debt crisis that threatened the integrity of the international financial system and robbed many of the developing countries of a decade of growth. The experience was sobering and demanded a reappraisal of many of the poli-

---

employees), capitalized at less than $3,000 (78 percent) usually supplied by the entrepreneur (71 percent). The majority of the entrepreneurs are men (90 percent) with little formal education (70 percent did not complete primary school, and 20 percent are illiterate) and no prior experience in enterprise management who are strongly integrated in the ethnic or family solidarity system.

On the average these enterprises have been operating for fewer than five years with no legal basis, except for the commerce sector (77 percent are officially registered). Only 10 percent have all infrastructure and amenities (water, electricity, and telephone), while 50 percent operate with none. However, the majority of these entrepreneurs intend to look for financing to invest in new equipment and infrastructure. In 1989 only 33 percent of these enterprises invested in additional equipment, of which 60 percent was in the service sector.

The study's recommendations to the government were to liberalize fiscal policy, including lowering taxes and increasing availability of small credit for investment in new equipment; to train entrepreneurs in management, including advice on how to keep their household finances separate from their business accounts; and to provide incentives for the formation of trade unions and entrepreneur associations.

Source: "Estudo de préviabilidade da promoçao e fomento da microempresa em Bissau" (Bissau: Ministério da Economia e Finanças, Republica da Guiné-Bissau, 1991).

cies that had led to the crisis. Unsound investments by the debtor countries and unwarranted lending by the commercial banks as well as by bilateral donors were among the contributing factors. Today, with hindsight, it is clear that much of the pain that accompanied the necessary restructuring of the countries' debt burden could have been avoided by a swifter response by the governments of those debtor countries and by an earlier recognition by the creditor countries that some exceptional measures to reduce the debt burden of the poorest countries was necessary.

Nevertheless, it is also clear that the management of the debt crisis in the 1980s did not lead to the collapse of the international financial system as had been predicted by many. But if the systemic risk has receded, many countries are still not out of the woods, and a new round of in-depth restructuring will be required, including substantial debt reduction for the poorest countries in Africa.

An important development of the 1990s, however, is that financial flows have started again from the OECD countries to the developing world. This time, however, the flows are private capital, which does not involve the creation of a public debt burden. This is a significant positive development, which shows that the pursuit of sound macroeconomic policies and the creation of an appropriate enabling environment are not only essential for growth, but also successfully attract foreign direct investment (FDI).

Just how important FDI can be is illustrated by a few figures. Private capital flows reached over $170 billion in 1994. Of these flows, about 45 percent were in the form of FDI. The remainder was debt and portfolio equity, but, as opposed to the commercial lending of the 1970s, it was mainly in the form of bond issues by about twenty of the more creditworthy countries. This represents a market test of the ability of these countries to access the capital markets again in a voluntary fashion due to renewed confidence following the reforms of their macroeconomic policies. The risk of defaults is therefore significantly less than it was in the 1980s. Nevertheless, it would be foolhardy to ignore the vulnerability of some of the eighteen countries that account for 80 percent of these flows, as the Mexican crisis of late 1994 showed. Some countries are accumulating liabilities at a faster rate than their export growth. Others are seeing a marked deterioration of their macroeconomic position. These are warning flags that must be watched to ensure that the errors of the past are not repeated (see box 3-15). On a more systemic level, concerns remain about the volatility of huge capital flows. This will require innovative and visionary thinking in the years ahead.

But the most important element in the emerging picture is the approximately $70 billion of annual FDI flowing from the industrial countries to the developing countries. The key issue to remember, however, is that these flows are susceptible to reversal if the policies that made them possible are not sustained. They are both a reward for past performance and an inducement to governments to stay the course of sound economic management. Success is the best instigator of further success.

Will FDI replace the need of the developing countries to receive formal ODA transfers? Undoubtedly for some middle-income countries this may well be the case, but FDI remains concentrated in a

---

Box 3-15. Lessons of the Debt Crisis

Preventing a crisis
• Prudent lending and borrowing policies should take into account vulnerability to external shocks.
• Building risk-sharing contingencies into financial contracts makes crises less likely, and less costly if they occur.
• External finance for low-income countries must come largely from official concessional sources.
Dealing with a crisis
• In a solvency crisis, early recognition of insolvency as the root cause and the need for final settlement are important in minimizing the damage.
• The final settlement of a solvency crisis requires debt and debt-service reduction.
• Good domestic policy is the basis for regularization of relations with external creditors.
• The official sector has an important role to play in implementing a final settlement and solving a crisis.

limited number of countries, unfortunately, and for the bulk of the poorest countries, it will not address the basic issues of investment in human resources and in the infrastructure so badly needed for the private sector to take off.

For the foreseeable future, therefore, we will need to see increasing flows of both ODA and FDI, although the former should be more targeted and concessional and the latter should broaden its scope of activities geographically and sectorally. However, FDI can only be encouraged and nurtured. It cannot be mandated. The governments and their development partners will therefore have to be imaginative in the design of their fiscal and trade regimes and unwavering in their support for the creation of the enabling environment conducive to sound private-sector investments. This will be an important part of the challenge of sound development policies in the future.

Reform: A Comprehensive, Long-Term Process

How does one move from distorted, inefficient bureaucratic economic management toward a market-friendly, human-centered development approach?

Effective reforms to promote sustainable development require actions on many fronts. It is not enough just to "get the prices right." Economic activity does not occur in a vacuum. The macro environment must be conducive, without excessive distortions or instabilities. Markets must be monitored. Ownership structures matter, and above all institutional structures and the quality of governance are essential to provide people the sense of confidence required to invest and produce.

Figure 3-16 summarizes the present consensus on the phasing of reforms based on the lessons learned from reforming economies worldwide. The time horizon is about ten years and could well take longer. The essential aspect is that movement in one area without the others is unlikely to be effective. Synergies exist among the various measures. The sequencing of the measures is equally important. Thus, for example, liberalizing trade without adjusting an overvalued exchange rate is likely to lead to a flood of imports without a proper supply response of domestic production and exports.

Figure 3-16. The Phasing of Reform

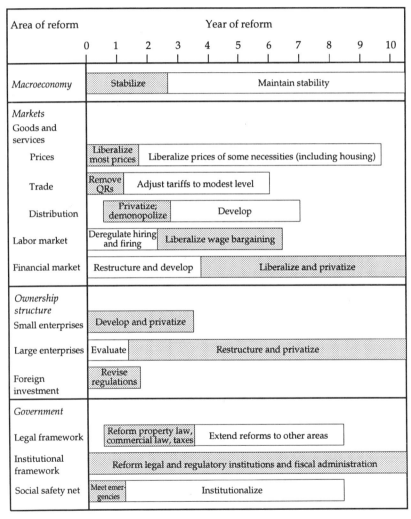

Note: Shading indicates intensive action. QRs are quantitative restrictions.
Source: World Bank, *World Development Report 1991: The Challenge of Development* (New York: Oxford University Press, 1991), 146.

Finally, the commitment of the authorities and the consistency of the application of the reform measures are important ingredients in the success of reform programs (box 3-16).

**Box 3-16. For Policymakers Everywhere:
Seven Lessons in Reform**

Successes provide the dos, failures the don'ts. The specifics of reform programs may vary across different regions and stages of development, but here are seven general pitfalls to avoid—or, on the flip side, seven lessons for better results.

• Lack of ownership undercuts the program. Programs initiated primarily because of the external financing that supported them, not because of conviction about their benefits, often have withered away for lack of government commitment to carry them through. For a program to be viewed as a country's own, nationals need to participate in its design and development. Building internal consensus is critical.

• Flip-flops in reform hurt credibility. Flexibility in policymaking is important, but when policies have been reversed capriciously— for example, when a tariff reform was soon followed by an import surcharge—the private sector has adopted a wait-and-see attitude. Subsequently, rather than responding energetically to a new reform, private agents act tentatively, if at all. Flexibility is important, yet bold, apparently irreversible steps by the government build confidence. They are especially needed in countries with a record of policy reversals.

• Institutional demands must not be glossed over. In many countries, ambitious changes could not be followed through because the country lacked trained personnel and adequate institutions: an independent judiciary, clearly defined and enforced property rights, and a strong central bank. Reform is a complex process of interwoven tasks, and there need to be mechanisms for interministerial coordination to carry them out. The development of institutional capacity needs to be emphasized from the outset because institution-building takes time and results will not be immediate. In the meantime, it helps to implement actions that economize on scarce capabilities— such as deregulating domestic markets, liberalizing agricultural marketing, and removing quantitative restrictions.

• Attention to macroeconomic instability is fundamental. Continuing fiscal imbalances can derail reforms. Severe macroeconomic instability has caused more than one trade and financial lib-

The Social Dimensions of Adjustment

Few issues have generated as much debate in the 1980s as the issue of the Social Dimensions of Adjustment (SDA). This was launched by a

eralization program to fail. In highly inflationary settings, up front and drastic reduction of the fiscal deficit is paramount. Many structural reforms can help: liberalizing agricultural marketing, switching from quantitative restrictions to tariffs, privatizing loss-making state enterprises, and improving tax administration.

• Vulnerable people must not be forgotten. The social costs of inaction are generally much larger than those of adjusting, but it is necessary to cushion the effect of adjustment on the most adversely affected groups. Cutbacks in public spending can hurt vulnerable groups. Reforms that allow agricultural prices to rise help poor farmers but often hurt the rural landless and urban poor. Thus, special programs of assistance to the poor are needed during the reform. Attention to politically powerful groups is also often necessary to sustain the changes. Finally, programs to compensate and retrain discharged civil servants are often needed when the public sector retrenches.

• Partial attempts often fail. When domestic deregulation did not accompany external liberalization, investment and output responded slowly. When trade reform did not accompany domestic deregulation, investment went to the wrong sectors. And when tariff reduction was not complemented by a broadening of the domestic tax base and a reduction in tax exemptions and subsidies, fiscal imbalances emerged, threatening the trade liberalization. There is thus a premium on taking simultaneous, complementary actions.

• It pays to be realistic. Policymakers and external agencies need to be realistic in preparing the financing plan to support reforms. Many countries may also need to reassign funds from low-priority to high-priority areas, for example, by switching some expenditures from the military to infrastructure and social programs. Realism also applies to expectations about what the reform is going to achieve. It pays not to promise too much too soon, yet to be loud and clear about the importance of reforming—and to contrast the outcome of reform with the alternative outcome of not reforming. Realistic expectations about the benefits and costs of the changes make the sustainability of the program more likely.

Source: World Bank, *World Development Report 1991: The Challenge of Development* (New York: Oxford University Press, 1991), 152.

number of academics and agencies (notably UNICEF) who were concerned that the early adjustment programs launched in the period
from 1979 to 1984 were excessively focused on macroeconomic stabi-

---

Box 3-17. The Social Dimensions of Adjustment program

The Social Dimensions of Adjustment (SDA) program began in 1987
as an attempt by multilateral agencies and donor governments to
find ways to assist poor and vulnerable groups affected by the
adjustment process in African countries. Donors and other agencies
channeled some $22 million through the World Bank between 1987
and 1992 to establish and operate the SDA program. The policy
agenda of the program comprised four lines of action. (1) Poverty
reduction concerns needed to be addressed in the formulation of
macroeconomic and sectoral policy, not as an add-on or after-
thought. (2) The virtual absence of any data with which to undertake economic analysis or distinguish the poor and their traits made
it imperative to collect accurate data on the living conditions of the
poor. This was essential both to design effective policies and targeted programs and to assess development over time. (3) Social action
programs and social funds needed to be designed and implemented
to address the needs of the vulnerable, especially those adversely
affected by the adjustment process. (4) There was the need to develop capacity locally to undertake poverty analysis and prepare
poverty-focused programs and follow up on their implementation.
These mutually reinforcing lines of action became the policy agenda
of the SDA program, as illustrated in box figure 3-17.
     Since the SDA began, thirty-three countries have asked to partici-
pate. Twenty-one country programs are either ongoing or at an
advanced state of preparation. Some eighteen donors and agencies,
along with local governments, have committed $253 million for the
implementation of these country programs. The African Heads of
State and Governments singled out this program for laudatory comment at their summit meeting of July 1990 in Addis Ababa (Resolution
AHG/Res. 8 [XXVI]). The World Bank has gradually mainstreamed
SDA activities within those of the Bank. The donors to the SDA program have requested that they continue to meet semiannually to look
into broad issues of poverty and social policy in Africa under the new
name of the Poverty and Social Policy Advisory Committee.

Source: African Development Bank, United Nations Development
Programme, and the World Bank, *The Social Dimensions of Adjustment in
Africa: A Policy Agenda* (Washington, D.C.: World Bank, 1990), 20.

lization, relied unduly on demand management, and had very short-term time horizons. Such programs, it was argued, would be recessionary and would put the bulk of the cost of adjustment on the poor and the vulnerable. There was much truth to these concerns, insofar as these early adjustment programs failed to take SDA into account. Yet the situation changed rapidly. By late 1983 the World Bank had concluded that adjustment, at least in Africa, was going to be a long-term affair. The 1984 report *Toward Sustained Development: A Joint Program of Action for Sub-Saharan Africa* called for a compact between donors and those countries that were willing to put their economic house in order for a sustained program of support.[58] Subsequently, the World Bank launched a formal program to take SDA fully into account (box 3-17), and the IMF and the World Bank support programs were made consistent with governments' medium-term (three-year) programs through a

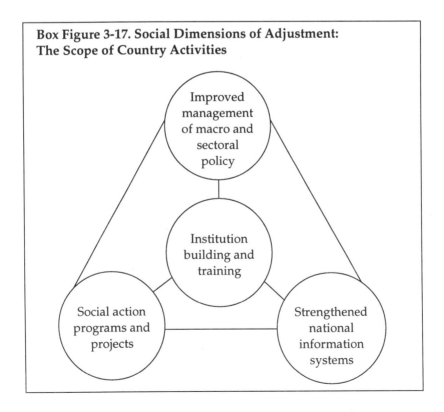

Box Figure 3-17. Social Dimensions of Adjustment: The Scope of Country Activities

Improved management of macro and sectoral policy

Institution building and training

Social action programs and projects

Strengthened national information systems

collective instrument called the Policy Framework Paper (PFP).

The SDA program grew rapidly in importance. Supported by a like-minded group of donors, it helped mobilize over $250 million for social action programs in diverse African countries undertaking structural adjustment. These programs varied in content depending on country needs, but they were intended to assist countries such as Uganda cope with their formidable social problems in periods of economic stringency and adjustment (box 3-18).

But SDA interventions were not just add-ons to the "main program." Far from it. They aimed at introducing the social dimension into the heart of the design of macroeconomic strategy. Clearly, the success of this objective varied from country to country, but it remains a primary objective being pursued by decisionmakers and development practitioners everywhere.

Box 3-18. Uganda: Programme for the Alleviation of Poverty and the Social Costs of Adjustment

As part of its Economic Recovery Programme, the government of Uganda has prepared a Programme for the Alleviation of Poverty and the Social Costs of Adjustment (PAPSCA). The PAPSCA consists of nineteen targeted initiatives at a total cost of $106 million, of which IDA will provide $28 million to finance two components and to strengthen the government's capacity to improve social policy planning.

The project will address some of the most pressing social concerns of Uganda's most vulnerable groups. In the short term it will use NGOs as implementing agencies to supplement the government's limited implementation capacity. The project will help local communities to improve primary education facilities by rehabilitating more than 4,000 classrooms in twelve of the most disadvantaged districts. The project also will develop assistance programs for widows and orphans—victims of war and AIDS—including basic health care, basic education (through scholarships, job skills training, and rehabilitation of rural training centers), and nutrition. In the Masindi District assistance will be provided to strengthen district health personnel and community-based health organiza-

Aid Coordination

If duplication, waste, and contradictions are to be avoided, the proliferation of international actors and the wide range of instruments needed for development assistance require considerable effort at aid coordination. Furthermore, the international partners concerned with development in a particular country must try to ensure that their collective input, both quantitative and qualitative, matches the beneficiary country's requirements in terms of timing and mix of aid, for example, balance of payments support, technical assistance, and project finance. This goal requires setting out mechanisms for coordination among many sovereign states and independent agencies. Consultative Groups (usually chaired by the World Bank) or Round Tables (usually chaired by UNDP) have been the preferred mechanisms. Recently, the special case of Sub-Saharan Africa has

---

tions. The access of urban residents living in hazardous environmental conditions to adequate water supply and sanitation facilities will also be improved through one of the project's components. The project will complement ongoing community initiatives by creating a mechanism to fund the materials, tools, and skilled labor required to maintain, rehabilitate, or construct wells, schools, health centers, and community access roads. These two subcomponents are expected to benefit approximately 400,000 people.

Through the component for social policy planning the project will strengthen the government's ability to design programs and policies to protect economically vulnerable groups from the transitory impact of adjustment and to facilitate their participation in the country's economic recovery. The component will provide short-term technical support to strengthen and develop social policy planning, a statistical data base (through a Priority Household Survey on the level and evolution of household socioeconomic conditions), and experience in designing and implementing actions to address the basic needs of Uganda's most disadvantaged groups.

Source: African Development Bank, United Nations Development Programme, and World Bank, *The Social Dimensions of Adjustment in Africa: A Policy Agenda* (Washington, D.C.: World Bank, 1990), 20.

triggered the most ambitious effort at donor coordination on a continental scale through what is known as the Special Program of Assistance for Africa (box 3-19).

But if aid coordination is imperative in terms of international transactions, it is no less important at the level of in-country implementation, where the multiplicity of donor agencies with

---

Box 3-19. Special Program of Assistance for Africa

Donors and creditors launched the three-year Special Program of Assistance for Africa (SPA) in late 1987 at the urging of the Development Committee as an extraordinary response to the problems facing countries in Africa. To be eligible for SPA assistance, countries must have low per capita income levels; they must be highly indebted; and they must be willing to implement policy reform programs for adjustment and growth. Since its inauguration the SPA has become the major mechanism for donors to mobilize and coordinate quick-disbursing aid and more concessional debt relief to support adjustment in Africa. At their October 1989 meeting SPA donors unanimously concurred to extend the program for another three years, from 1991 to 1993. The 1988–90 phase is known as SPA1; the 1991–93 phase is SPA2. SPA3, covering 1994–96, was launched in October 1993.

Twenty-three Sub-Saharan African countries initially received assistance from SPA during SPA1, but two (Somalia and Zaire) later became ineligible because of weak reform efforts. As of October 1993 a total of thirty-one countries were eligible.

The SPA donors meet semiannually to review the financing situation of member countries meeting with the aim of financing gaps in adjusting countries with increased disbursements. Cofinancing pledges are one of five components that comprise the resources within the SPA framework. The others are: IDA lending; supplemental IDA adjustment credits; resources from the IMF's structural adjustment facilities; and debt relief. SPA has mobilized $17.5 billion under SPA1. The donors agreed to US$23.4 billion in financing needs for 27 countries in SPA2 (assuming all countries' reform programs were on track), and have targeted US$34.7 billion for SPA3. It is estimated that of this assistance will be untied. Efforts are

their varying administrative requirements can paralyze already weak government agencies. One promising approach to both coordinate aid and streamline administrative procedures during implementation is exemplified by the Tanzanian Integrated Roads Project (box 3-20).

---

being made to increase the efficiency of disbursement of these resources through harmonizing and simplifying procurement procedures and encouraging transparency and accountability in the use of funds.

The SPA has shown that development efforts can be made more effective through joint action. There has been a strong demand to broaden the range of SPA activities. Although SPA resources remain focused in support of adjustment, SPA meetings are becoming fora for discussions of broader issues associated with adjustment. The issues on tha SPA-3 agenda include integrating poverty reduction measures into reform programs and public expenditure allocations, coordinating support for sector investment programs, and strengthening local management and institutional capacity.

The strong donor support for SPA stems from the evidence that domestic policy reforms coupled with adequate financial provisions substantially improve economic performance. For a typical country in the second half of the 1980s, exports grew as fast as they did during 1966 to 1979, and GDP grew faster. However, economic recovery in SPA countries has been diluted by rapid population growth and adverse movements in their terms of trade. If population growth had been contained at 1980–85 rates and the terms of trade had remained unchanged, per capita incomes would have grown at 0.9 percent per year during the second half of the 1980s instead of barely increasing.

The performance of SPA countries can also be evaluated in relation to other groups of low- and middle-income countries. For the period 1986 to 1991 the aggregate growth rates of GDP and gross domestic investment of SPA economies exceeded those of other regions except Asia. This upturn contrasts sharply with the period from 1966 to 1979, when all indicators of SPA economic performance were the lowest in the developing world.

**Box 3-20. Tanzania Integrated Roads Project:
A Unique Experiment in Complex Project Implementation**

At the end of the 1980s the World Bank began to finance new-style "integrated transport projects" in Burkina Faso, Ghana, Senegal, and Tanzania. The Tanzania Integrated Roads Project (IRP) presents an exceptional example of streamlining administrative procedures to speed up implementation in difficult field circumstances. The total cost for the first phase of the program is about $870 million, with financing for over 95 percent already committed or pledged from sixteen donors, making this the largest and most complex integrated road rehabilitation project in Africa. More than $50 million has been set aside for institutional development and policy reform, important elements for success.

The project is assisting the government to (1) develop strong management and technical capacity to operate, manage, and maintain the road infrastructure and transport services by providing well-focused training at all levels; and (2) transform the Ministry of Works (MOW) from a construction-oriented (blue collar) ministry to an administration and contract management-oriented (white collar) ministry, with the private sector construction industry doing the actual maintenance. Steps have been taken to institute a new organizational framework and to ensure effective coordination of donors and government, which are critical for prompt, efficient implementation. Performance budgeting is being installed to increase operational efficiency and ensure proper accountability.

The new organizational framework has been implemented in the MOW for planning, managing, and maintaining the road network, and greater executive responsibility for carrying out the works has been delegated to the ministry's twenty Regional Engineer's Offices (REOs). The REOs are responsible for delivering the agreed physical targets for road rehabilitation and maintenance. Quarterly budgets are only released once performance for the previous quarter and programs for the coming quarter have been approved. To simplify the process, procurement authority levels have been increased for the regional engineers, and simplified payment procedures have been introduced. Interim changes have been made in procurement regulations and supply management procedures for larger centralized contracts, and a study has been carried out to recommend comprehensive reform of the procurement system. A UNDP-financed Principal Transport Engineer and Project Coordinator has been instrumental in building bridges between government ministries and agencies and ensuring effective coordination of the sixteen donors.

With responsibility for the execution of works delegated to the REOs, capacity for maintaining the road network is being improved by strengthening the local contracting industry. All rehabilitation and an increasing amount of the maintenance are now carried out by contract. A construction industry development strategy aimed at local contractors, both big and small, is in place. Local contractors already have won two international competitive bidding (ICB) contracts worth about $23 million and an additional twelve local competitive bidding (LCB) contracts for road rehabilitation and maintenance works. At the other extreme, in several regions payments are being made to small truck operators to haul gravel for road maintenance.

Staff motivation is essential for increasing accountability. Within the ministry limited incentive payments have already been used very effectively, and a more comprehensive scheme is being designed and implemented. Career development is a central focus of personnel policy, with emphasis on assignments in the regions. A significant training program includes selective Master of Science and engineering diploma courses and courses in information technology, accounting, and management for senior management.

Mid-term review of this project took place in November 1992. The long-term goal in ensuring the success of the project is to further decentralize road management responsibilities and develop a strategy for the management of district and village roads.

Military Expenditures

One additional topic that deserves special attention here is military expenditures. Not only is there a trade-off between military expenditures and development, but this trade-off operates at three separate but interlinked levels:

• *At the level of the OECD countries.* The massive expenditures on the military during the cold war, which continue to this day, take away from potential spending on social and physical infrastructure in the North. They also promote a view of global security that relies on military muscle rather than the promotion of global well-being.[59] The end of the Cold War should provide an opportunity to reassess the security value to the North of improving levels of well-being in the poorer countries of the South.

• *At the level of financial flows.* Arms sales continue to be an important part of global trade and "aid" (see table 3-2).

• *At the level of the developing countries.* There is, to be sure, a legitimate need to provide for defense in all countries, but the level of expenditures on the military—compared to social—spending seems very high for many countries (see table 3-3). Furthermore, in most developing countries, the military has tended to become the governing elite, or at least an important part of it. The example of Costa

Table 3-2. Comparison of Military Expenditures, Aid, and Trade Levels, 1980–88

(billions of U.S. dollars)

	World	Industrial countries	Developing countries
Economic aid given			
1980	40.0	29.9	10.1
1988	55.7	53.1	2.6
Arms imports			
1980	35.0	8.2	26.8
1988	48.1	13.6	34.5
Arms exports			
1980	35.5	34.1	1.4
1988	48.9	43.5	5.4
Total merchandise imports[a]			
1980	1,946	1,369	577
1988	2,772	2,070	702
Total merchandise exports[a,b]			
1980	1,896	1,240	656
1988	2,690	1,983	707

a. Figures include reported arms trade.
b. Exports plus freight and insurance should approximate imports.
Source: For data on aid and arms, Ruth Leger Sivard, *World Military and Social Expenditures 1991*, 14th ed. (Washington, D.C.: World Priorities, 1991), 50. For data on merchandise imports and exports, IMF, Bureau of Statistics, *Direction of Trade Statistics Yearbook 1987* (Washington, D.C., IMF, 1987); and IMF, Bureau of Statistics, *Direction of Trade Statistics Yearbook 1992* (Washington, D.C., IMF, 1992).

Rica, which has formally abolished its military, is instructive: Costa Rica leads Latin America in many indicators of social and human development.

Despite the clear trade-offs, and the historical arguments about "guns and butter"—of which the public was constantly reminded by dedicated researchers[60] and NGOs—the subject of military expenditures was not formally tackled in the work of mainstream development agencies because of its overtly political nature. Former World Bank President Barber B. Conable put the issue squarely on the table in his address to the Board of Governors (the finance ministers of the world) in 1989 when he said:

> While there is much variation among developing countries, as a group low-income countries currently allocate around 20 percent of central government budgets to defense. In the mid-1980s military spending in developing countries exceeded spending on health and education combined. While many components of national budgets have been cut, the $200 billion which the developing world spends annually on the military has largely been protected. And arms are often a prime source of external debt: military debt accounts for a third or more of total debt service in several large developing countries.
>
> Developing countries on one side, and their arms suppliers and creditors on the other, must adapt to a world where budgets are tight. It is important to place military spending decisions on the same footing as other fiscal decisions, to examine possible trade-offs more systematically, and to explore ways to bring military spending into better balance with development priorities. In evaluating their military expenditures, governments should be realistic, but they also should remember the human consequences of these choices.[61]

For an intergovernmental institution like the World Bank to tackle such a delicate issue, however, raised important philosophical, conceptual, operational, and statutory questions.[62] This

90   NURTURING DEVELOPMENT

author was an early protagonist of addressing these issues, albeit with care and realism.[63] Others have addressed these issues in the context of development and development assistance.[64] Robert McNamara suggested that donors limit aid to countries spending

Table 3-3. Public Expenditure on the Military Compared with Social Sectors, 1986
(percentage of GNP)

Military expenditure	Expenditure on health and education			
	.....1.0–1.9.....	....................................2.0–4.9..............................		
Less than 1.		Brazil Ghana	Mexico	Niger
1.0–1.9	Nigeria Paraguay	Argentina Bangladesh Cameroon Colombia Dominican Rep.	Ecuador Guatemala Haiti Nepal Philippines	Romania Rwanda Sierra Leone
2.0–4.9	Uganda Zaire	Burundi Benin Bolivia Burkina Faso	El Salvador Guinea India Indonesia	Mali Myanmar Turkey Uruguay
5.0–9.9		Chad China Pakistan	Peru Sri Lanka Sudan	United Arab Emirates
10.0 and above		Angola	Iraq	

Note: The ranges given in this table are illustrative of the differences in expenditures in the different categories; they are not necessarily indicative of precise differences across countries because of some differences in definition. The estimates of social expenditure do not cover those made by local bodies.

more than 2 percent of GNP on defense, except under exceptional circumstances.[65] Others have also been struggling with ways in which this topic could be effectively addressed by aid donors.[66] Whatever the outcome, it is now clear that the issue is finally making its appearance in a serious and sustained manner in the

Expenditure on health and education				
......5.0–9.9......			......10.0 and above......	
Barbados	Cyprus	The Gambia	Costa Rica	Luxembourg
Algeria	Jamaica	Trinidad and Tobago	Austria	Japan
Central African Rep.	Malta	Venezuela	Finland	Switzerland
Côte d'Ivoire	Papua New Guinea		Ireland	
Fiji	Swaziland			
Bulgaria	Kenya	South Africa	Australia	Netherlands
Chile	Lesotho	Spain	Belgium	New Zealand
Congo	Liberia	Tanzania	Botswana	Norway
Czechoslovakia	Madagascar	Thailand	Canada	Panama
Gabon	Malawi	Togo	Denmark	Portugal
German Dem. Rep.	Mauritania	Yugoslavia	France	Sweden
Hungary	Poland	Zambia	Germany, Fed. Rep.	
Italy	Senegal			
	Somalia			
Bahrain	Honduras	Singapore	United Kingdom	Zimbabwe
Cuba	Korea, Rep. of	Tunisia		
Egypt	Kuwait	United States		
Ethiopia	Malaysia	Yemen, Arab Rep.		
Greece	Morocco			
Iran, I.R. of	Oman	Yemen, P.D.R.	Guyana	Nicaragua
Israel	Syria		Libya	Saudi Arabia
Jordan	USSR			

Source: World Bank, *World Development Report 1991: The Challenge of Development* (New York: Oxford University Press, 1991), 142.

Box 3-21. Military Expenditures and Developmental Interventions

The costs of ever-more-lethal armaments have skyrocketed during the last fifty years. Consider these unit costs:[a]

Unit costs of selected military equipment
(millions of U.S. dollars)

	1985	1993
1 tank (M-1 Abrams)	2.6	3.4
1 attack helicopter (Apache) (AH 64)	12.9	16.8
1 fighter aircraft (F-15)	32.8	42.9
1 fighter aircraft (F-18 E/F)	46.2	60.3
1 transport aircraft (C-17)	109.9	261.1
1 guided missile cruiser (Ticonderoga class) (CG-47)	878.6	1,147.0
1 aircraft carrier (CVN-76)	2,726.5	3,561.0

The cost of the expensive machinery of modern warfare could have major alternative uses if the financiers of armaments were willing to finance other uses. Consider:

Unit costs of selected development interventions
(U.S. dollars)

	1985[b]	1993[c]
1 oral rehydration treatment for 1 person, per incidence		
• Production cost	.06	.07
• Commercial cost	.07	.08
Parasite infection treatment for 1 primary student for 1 year[b]	.20–.40	.25–.50
Textbooks and writing materials for 1 primary student for 1 year[b]	2–15	2.50–19
Average primary school teacher salary for 1 year[b]	1,000–1,600	1,260–2,014
1 hand-dug well serving 350–400 people	3,000–5,000	3,000–5,000
1 borehole, cost to drill, serving 350–400 people	12,000–15,000	12,000–15,000

a. Center for Defense Information, Washington, D.C., March 1993 data. Costs include research and development.

b. Marlaine E. Lockheed and Adriaan M. Verspoor, with others, *Improving Primary Education in Developing Countries* (New York: Oxford University Press, 1991), 87, 367. Costs are for all low-income economies.

c. 1993 figures are calculated by inflating 1985 figures.

international development debate. New types of aid may have to be imagined, for example, in assisting with demobilization efforts after wars[67] as well as with reconstruction efforts that have long been supported by the international community.[68] At any rate, the opportunity cost of military expenditures is clear (see box 3-21).

The Importance of Democracy and Human Rights

Previous sections put the discussion of democracy and human rights in the context of the direct or indirect link that could be established with conventionally accepted objectives of development policy, such as reducing infant mortality or accelerating economic growth. That discussion emphasized the promotion of good governance in terms of increased transparency, accountability, pluralism, participation, and respect for the rule of law.

This was not a fully satisfactory treatment of a very important subject. Yet, it probably represents the most extensive interpretation of current mandates of most international and multilateral institutions dealing with development assistance from a purely technical perspective. These institutions, including all IFIs (except the EBRD), have statutory limits on the extent to which they may take on country issues that have a clear political dimension. Such restrictions do not apply in the case of bilateral assistance or private organizations.

The issues of democracy and human rights are so important that they warrant a different line of argument. I would argue that democracy and human rights should be pursued as intrinsically desirable objectives, regardless of whether they contribute to development as it is conventionally defined.[69]

Respect for human rights lies at the core of human well-being.[70] One could conceive of a society of well-fed, healthy, well-educated slaves, but surely no one would argue that such an outcome is an acceptable objective of our collective development efforts. The strongest arguments in favor of democracy flow from the proposition that we know of no reliable alternative form of government that is as likely to protect individuals from abuse of their basic human rights.[71]

Whatever the alleged inefficiencies of democratic decisionmaking processes, they do ensure some measure of accountability. By encouraging dissent, democratic decisionmaking, with its checks and balances, also protects against dramatic mistakes. Two observations support this contention:

First, no major loss of life from famine has occurred in a democratic country. Despite India's crushing poverty, outright famine has been successfully averted. Questions remain about the political system's ability to effectively reduce poverty, with its concomitant hunger and malnutrition, but that is different from what we now know to have happened in China in the late 1950s, even though China's subsequent achievements in massive poverty reduction remain unmatched.[72]

Second, in this century of wars and killing, it is striking that no two countries with established democratic systems have fought a war against each other.

If democracy and human rights are generally accepted as desirable, what are the possibilities of promoting them in the international arena?

Within the framework of development assistance, we should at least ensure that the development programs being supported tend to promote participation and the civil society that we know are conducive to good governance and ultimately to the promotion of greater respect for human rights. A comprehensive examination of effective and far-reaching action to promote democracy and human rights is beyond the scope of this essay; nevertheless, one can advance some suggestions.

On Sovereignty

The present international order is founded on the concept of state sovereignty. Sovereignty is defined as:
- Supreme power, especially over a body politic
- Freedom from external control, autonomy
- Controlling influence
- One that is sovereign, especially an autonomous state.[73]

This concept is the basis of almost all aspects of the international order. It implies reciprocal noninterference in internal affairs and respect for the territorial integrity of states and of internationally recognized frontiers.

The corollary of sovereignty is the recognition of the right of governments that exercise this "supreme power over a body politic" and are presumed to be able to exercise their "controlling influence" over the affairs of the societies within the territorial boundaries of the "sovereign state" in "freedom from external control" to enjoy "autonomy." Furthermore, the international order is based on a network of diplomatic and other relations among such governments. Formal channels for contacts and dialogue exist for almost all aspects of intercourse among nations through these channels among governments. Indeed, all undertakings that commit societies economically, militarily, politically, and even on such issues such as cultural exchanges and human rights, are entered into by governments, not by some undefined society at large.

While these arrangements may be unsatisfactory, they appear, like democracy, to be the least harmful of all known forms of international arrangements for organizing relations between peoples and nations. One should therefore approach any questions breaching sovereignty with a great deal of caution.

Aside from the pragmatic "least-harmful" criterion, the philosophical justification of sovereignty is found in the recognition of the differences among human societies and the inalienable right of each society to organize itself in the manner that suits it best—the formalistic expression of peoples' rights to self-determination and to freedom from another people's imposition upon them of an order to which they do not subscribe. This, of course, was the basis of decolonization, independence, and accession of many states to full membership in the community of nations. It also raises issues about the rights of minorities to secede from existing states and a host of thorny questions associated with the relationships between sovereign states and minorities within the boundaries of other sovereign states.

More pertinent to our discussion is that sovereignty is subject to certain internationally recognized constraints such as respect for human rights. Such constraints, are enshrined in international instruments to which governments have committed their sovereign states.[74] There are also questions about the legitimacy or representativeness of existing governments, which lead to issues of de facto and de jure recognition of governments, usually as a result of conflicting changes of authority within a sovereign state. There is only one notable case in which the legitimacy of a government within a sovereign state was impugned because of its systemic (not just systematic) violation of human rights, and that is the Republic of South Africa and the General Assembly's vote on the issue of apartheid.[75]

It is noteworthy, however, that while impugning the representativeness or legitimacy of the government in charge, these debates have not questioned the issue of sovereignty per se and have sought to remedy the situation by using diplomatic and economic sanctions. These were debated and adopted within the existing international framework, that is, within and by the community of sovereign states. Indeed, one can see in this the legitimating process for conflict resolution.

Hence, in seeking through external intrusion to breach the sovereignty of states on issues as political, sensitive, and judgmental as the representativeness of an elected government or the boundaries between repression and legitimate, maintainable law and order, some questions as to the *desirability* and *effectiveness* of such an intrusion must be raised.

Breaching Sovereignty

Sovereignty is not inviolable.[76] Indeed, the UN sanctions against South Africa illustrate that the community of nations can find the internal behavior of a state (in this case, apartheid) to be so contrary to the fundamental values of civilized behavior (in this case, respect for human rights) that some collective action (in this case, sanctions) is justified. These criteria provide the framework for collective action breaching sovereignty. The key elements are:

• Anchoring the basis for judgment and subsequent action in a document that is widely recognized as having universal or regional authority and to which the state in question is a party. Examples of documents having universal authority are the UN Charter, the UN Declaration of Human Rights,[77] and the Geneva Conventions. The European Community Charter for the EC member states is an example of a document having regional authority.

• Having a recognized mechanism by which collective action could be decided on and implemented. This is important if unilateral intervention in other states' affairs is to be avoided. The UN Security Council is an example of such a mechanism. The European model with a parliament and a separate commission is a regional and more far-reaching example. It is essential that the legitimation of collective action be rooted in the legality of a process to which all the relevant states have agreed in advance.

This approach is far preferable to anything that would leave difficult questions of governance, human rights, destabilization, and security to be dealt with at the level of bilateral relations, if at all.

International institutions could then agree to support an international or a regional consensus within the limits of their statutes if their governing boards agree to do so. This approach would have the merit of putting the onus for identifying egregious behavior on the collective decisions of the member states. They could then, as members of their international institutions, argue at their boards for support of their collective international or regional decisions, to the extent that these are consistent with their institutional statutes. This process would remove the confrontational and judgmental aspect that a unilateral action by the staff of international agencies would engender.

The preceding does not mean that those concerned with development should do nothing. General advocacy of better governance by the international institutions can be very effective and does not require any change in statutes. To the extent that one follows the path of advocacy, dialogue, and supportive action, the slippery slope of unilateral political conditionality will be avoided. It is far better to strengthen the hand of domestic, endogenous reform movements by force of argument and international support than to try to impose changes from the outside, especially when they have not gained the formal support of collective international action.

Empowerment of the Poor

We have referred several times to empowerment of the poor as the key to successful and sustainable development. The substance of empowerment lies in enabling those among the poor who do not have access to assets to acquire them. Assets, especially in rural agrarian societies, primarily mean land. Empowerment also implies increasing the returns on the assets held by the poor, primarily their labor (through investments in health, education, and training), as well as other assets such as land and equipment (through provision of credit and extension). All of this has to be done within a general framework conducive to supporting private, small-scale initiative: an enabling environment.

Why has this not happened? Largely because the institutional structures of government and the formal institutions of the modern economy in most developing countries have not placed a high priority on reaching the poor. They have frequently claimed that the administrative costs of dealing with microenterprises was prohibitive and that the poor were a bad credit risk. Both of these contentions have been effectively challenged by the example of the Grameen Bank of Bangladesh (box 3-22). This bank has successfully extended credit to the poorest of the poor, over 1.5 million of them, almost all landless rural women. With loans averaging $100 or less, Grameen has a repayment rate of 98 percent, considerably better than most "development banks" that lend to well-off entrepreneurs in the developing countries.

Empowerment of the poor is not a slogan raised by idealistic NGOs or by political demagogues. It is a feasible reality, although it remains all too rare. At present, examples of successfully replicated schemes reaching a large number of individuals, such as the Grameen Bank, are few and far between. The paucity of other successes can in part be explained by the shortage of persons with the unique qualities of Dr. Muhammad Yunus, visionary founder of the Grameen Bank. One can only hope that his example will encourage many others to dedicate their lives to making similar dreams a reality. In part, it is because of

Box 3-22. Empowering the Poorest of the Poor:
The Grameen Bank of Bangladesh

The Grameen Bank serves the needs of the poorest of the poor on this planet. The landless rural women of Bangladesh account for the vast bulk (93 percent) of the bank's approximately 1.5 million borrowers, and they are also its owners. Currently, the Grameen Bank lends $20 million each month and is working in 32,000 of the 68,000 villages in Bangladesh. The bank provides loans averaging $100 and enjoys a repayment rate averaging 98 percent—far better than most "development banks" lending to entrepreneurs in the developing countries.

The Grameen Bank is the result of the dedication of a visionary economist: Dr. Muhammad Yunus, who founded the bank and, against all odds, has imbued its 12,000 employees with the same sense of mission and the same dedication to service that motivates him. The success of the Grameen enterprise is a lesson that the most formidable obstacles yield to determination. It is a testimonial to what confidence in the empowerment of the weak and the marginalized can achieve.

Not only do the Grameen borrowers repay their loans, they prosper. One follow-up study has shown that most Grameen borrowers take additional loans after repaying their initial loans and improve their income levels by as much as 35 percent per year. More important, Grameen Bank assists its members in finding self-respect and dignity and in becoming agents of development in their immediate communities. Grameen members adopt a sixteen-point self- and community-improvement program, which appears to be highly effective. Grameen provides additional services to its members, including some insurance for decent burial and exceptional assistance through mutual support in times of personal or family crises.

Some argue that Grameen's operations, or at least its programs for expanding its network, are not viable without a slight subsidy. Whatever the merits of this argument, this writer can think of few more deserving avenues for spending public and international funds than supporting Grameen and deserving enterprises modeled after it in other countries.

In an area in which most government programs have failed and in which few NGOs have succeeded in expanding the scale of their operations, Grameen, banker to the poorest of the poor, is a signal success deserving recognition and praise.

the absence of an enabling environment in most developing countries. It is here that development assistance has a role to play in nurturing this enabling environment that will empower the poor and the marginalized to become the producers of their own welfare. Whether development aid is reoriented in this direction will be a major factor in increasing the effectiveness of development assistance in the 1990s.

Involuntary Resettlement

As we discuss the empowerment of the poor, it is important to recognize that routine developmental activities can lead to the disempowerment and impoverishment of people. This is the result of involuntary resettlement of populations for large infrastructure projects. The World Bank has been a leader in calling attention to this problem, and was the first international agency to adopt a formal policy on the subject in 1980 (see box 3-23). A recent report by the World Bank[78] estimated that every year construction projects like dams, power stations, and irrigation and transportation systems in developing nations lead to the involuntary resettlement of more than 10 million people, many of whom lose their land and income.

Projects financed by World Bank loans account for less than 3 percent of involuntary resettlements for development around the world. By and large, those 3 percent are treated far better than others, although not as well as we would hope.

Involuntary resettlement has been the unpleasant consequence of modernization in the developed and developing world. Building large-scale projects has always created resettlement problems, from the Tennessee Valley dams of the United States to the Aswan Dam of Egypt, but the benefits can be spectacular. For example, the multipurpose Xiaolandgdi Dam, under construction in China, will create about $500 million annually in irrigation, flood and sediment control, and power. Those economic benefits will increase up to $900 million a year in the dam's thirtieth year. The Xiaolandgdi Dam will protect 103 million people living in the flood plain of the Yellow River Basin. This project is resettling 181,000 people at a cost of $570 million—about one fourth the cost of building the dam, but just slightly more than the economic benefits from only its first year of operation.

Disruptive as they can be in densely settled countries, large-scale infrastructure projects are absolutely necessary. More than 2 billion

---

Box 3-23. The Bank's Resettlement Policy

• Involuntary displacement should be avoided or minimized whenever feasible, because of its disruptive and impoverishing effects.

• Where displacement is unavoidable, the objective of Bank policy is to assist displaced persons in their efforts to improve former living standards and earning capacity, or at least to restore them. The means to achieve the Bank's objective consist of preparing and executing resettlement plans as development programs. These resettlement programs are integral parts of project designs.

• Displaced persons should be (a) compensated for their losses at replacement cost, (b) given opportunities to share in project benefits, and (c) assisted with the transfer and, during the transition period, at the relocation site.

• Moving people in familiar groups can cushion disruptions. Minimizing the distance between departure and relocation sites can facilitate the resettlers' adaptation to the new sociocultural and natural environments. The trade-offs between distance and economic opportunities must be balanced carefully.

• Resettlers' participation in planning resettlement should be promoted. The existing social and cultural institutions of resettlers and their hosts should be relied upon in conducting the transfer and reestablishment process.

• New communities of resettlers should be designed as viable settlement systems equipped with infrastructure and services, able to be integrated in the regional economic context.

• Host communities that receive resettlers should be assisted to overcome possible adverse social and environmental effects from increased population density.

• Indigenous people, ethnic minorities, pastoralists, and other groups that may have informal customary rights to the land or other resources taken for the project must be provided with adequate land, infrastructure, and other compensation. The absence of formal legal title to land by such groups should not be grounds for denying them compensation and rehabilitation.

people worldwide still lack access to electricity and are forced to use sticks and dung for their energy needs, 1.7 billion lack sewerage systems, and 1 billion lack access to clean, piped water, resulting in the deaths of 2 million to 3 million infants and children each year.

On a per capita basis, the rich countries are consuming an average of 30 times more energy than the low-income developing countries. But the developing countries' economies are growing fast, especially in East Asia, and population pressures are dramatic in most parts of the developing world, particularly in cities. It is inconceivable that these citizens would not get more electricity, transport, and services, all of which require investments in infrastructure. In this regard, small-scale, nondisruptive technologies offer limited scope. The moment certain thresholds—for example, urban densities of 400 persons per hectare—are crossed, proper sewerage and sanitation systems connected to treatment plants are needed. While every effort must be made to minimize involuntary displacement and resettlement, it is impossible to eliminate it completely. The population densities of most developing countries are very high. For instance, Bangladesh, with 120 million persons, covers an area about the size of Arkansas, which has only 2.5 million inhabitants.

So the key is to minimize resettlement hardship through better designs and to assist the resettled population in restarting their lives. Compassion is called for when dealing with those resettled, because people are uprooted from their traditional lands, and their life-styles are disrupted. Resettlement, which can be devastating, has to be handled with humane concern for those affected, and a dedication to achieving the reconstitution of the income-earning capacities of the resettled populations.

Bank experience shows that if a government adopts its own (national) policy to reintegrate displaced people into the national economy, resettlement is successful for more than just Bank-financed projects. Piecemeal, halfhearted attempts to deal with resettlement by uncommitted governments do not work. For example, China has adopted an approach based on its emphasis on employment. Whenever people must be involuntarily resettled, the government commits itself to finding work for them, with responsibility

delegated to local officials who know the situation best. This process
has worked very well (box 3-24).

The key to sound resettlement is to adopt a people-centered development approach, not a property-compensation approach. The
World Bank is encouraging governments to adopt such an
approach. For example, in one 1990 project, 2,800 people in 500

Box 3-24. China's Shuikou Hydropower Dam

The first Bank-assisted project in China involving resettlement to
which the Bank's guidelines on resettlement were fully applied was
the Shuikou Hydropower Dam project, located on the Min River. It
is a model for many subsequent projects that require resettlement
with which the Bank is assisting in China.

The Shuikou project involved relocating 88 villages belonging to 15
townships in three counties, and large parts of Nanping City, dis-
placing 20,000 households, with about 68,000 rural and urban people.

The Chinese government invested years of staff time working on
the resettlement, with the Bank assisting. Planning put the main
emphasis on restoring the productive capacity of those being resettled, bringing new land into cultivation for them, creating jobs or
new commercial opportunities, providing new housing with more
floor space per capita, and providing new social amenities.

Detailed provisions were included in the project appraisal report
and a legal agreement with specific provisions about resettlement
was concluded between the Bank and the Chinese government. The
project started in 1987 and the first 1,400 resettlers from the dam's
site moved to new houses by the end of 1988.

By the beginning of 1993, six years into project implementation,
about 67,200 people—or 98.8 percent of the total—had been moved
to similar or better housing. With the housing compensation and
materials received—timber, cement, and iron—villagers have been
able to hire their own contractors and build for themselves new and
better housing.

Breadwinners from families comprising 38,000 people have got-
ten new jobs as well.

Moving people only short distances and building new and better-
constructed schools has preserved many, if not all, social ties and family linkages. These connections have helped to cushion difficulties.

"squatter" families were to be involuntarily resettled. They were living near a river channel scheduled for widening. Compensation would have been about $35 per household. Because of Bank objections, the government withdrew the project from World Bank financing, leaving the families with inadequate compensation. In contrast, a similar project in Indonesia (Semarang Drainage Improvement Program) was part of a Bank-assisted program. It entailed the displacement of 13,000 people in 2,230 families, of whom only 113 had clear legal title to their land. About 1,900 families were eventually relocated. The Bank's appraisal mission had successfully negotiated the application of Bank policy to this effort. The resettled receive, in addition to cash compensation, land, services, and infrastructure. Most important, regardless of their former status, all those relocated were given title to their new land.

Several countries and agencies have now adopted resettlement policies that parallel those of the Bank. These include the following:

Brazil. In 1990, the state-run energy company, Electrobras, approved resettlement guidelines similar to the Bank's for the nation's power sector. These guidelines are intended to be used for all 36 new hydroelectric plants in the 1990–99 government plan, not just for the two or three dams cofinanced by the Bank. The Brazilian government agency in charge of approving new development plans has already terminated plans for four projects because they would have required the involuntary resettlement of between 154,000 and 188,000 people.

The Philippines. The Philippines Urban Development and Housing Act of 1992 restricts displacement and mandates participation and consultation policies to help those who have to be forcibly resettled. It is one of the few such laws in effect in any country.

Turkey. The government passed a clear law regulating resettlement, and Turkey has been open to policy dialogues with the Bank and receptive to improving its existing legal provisions. Because of this formal legal framework and the recent improvements in its application, the government is able to allocate substantial financial resources to resettlement.

India. Following negotiations with the Bank, India's National

Thermal Power Corporation (NTPC) adopted a Resettlement and Rehabilitation Policy in 1993 for all its operations, which set an important precedent for that sector. The policy emphasizes the principle of income restoration and guarantees specific entitlements to resettlers not previously provided in displacements caused by NTPC projects.

Gujarat State, India. Extensive negotiation between the Bank and the government of Gujarat over serious problems affecting the implementation of the Narmada Sardar Sarovar project have resulted in significant improvements in Gujarat's legal regulations for resettlement, which now formally grants displaced people certain important entitlements. These improved regulations, however, apply only to the specific project and not to similar ongoing projects in Gujarat State.

Adoption of sound resettlement policies and approaches requires avoiding involuntary resettlement whenever feasible, and where unavoidable, reducing its magnitude. Some significant examples follow.

Indonesia. The Bank policy produced a workable compromise between the government's desire for optimum power capacity for the Saguling Dam project and the need to reduce involuntary resettlement among people living near the project. The redesign of the initial engineering proposal lowered dam height from 650 to 645 meters, reducing displacement from 90,000 to 55,000 people, with only a small loss of power.

Thailand. Resiting of the Pak Mun Dam from a location that would have displaced more than 20,000 people to an alternative site has reduced displacement to about 4,000 people.

Ecuador. The redesign of canal layouts in the Guayas Flood Control Project has lowered displacement from more than 3,000 people to none at all.

China. The Shanghai Sewerage Project, by using tunnels rather than surface channels to lay pipes and by resiting the main pipeline, reduced the anticipated resettlement from 2,700 to 1,400 households.

Côte d'Ivoire. The government's initial proposal for the Forestry Sector Project, if accepted, would have displaced 100,000 to 200,000 people. Alternative approaches lowered this number to 40,000 people and set substantively different and improved standards for their location.

Working on the Long-Term Issues:
The Example of Agricultural Research

Many problems of development are so pressing that we are tempted to concentrate all our efforts on immediate action. Long-term issues tend to be shunted aside in the pursuit of immediate impact. Yet the environmental problems that we are witnessing today are the result of inadequate attention to these matters a generation ago, and many of the key developmental issues are of a long-term nature. Patient and consistent effort will be required for many years before the full effect of such important investments will be seen. Such investments are nonetheless pressing. Population, education, and global environmental issues are but some of the more obvious ones.

Less obvious, but as important for the developing countries, is agricultural research. Agriculture is an essential sector in developing countries both for promoting growth and for reducing poverty and hunger. Agriculture is the area where the interface between human activity and the environment is most pervasive, for both good and ill. Bad agricultural practices lead to soil erosion, deforestation, pollution from the excessive use of pesticides and fertilizers, and impoverishment. Good agricultural practices can conserve biodiversity, protect the natural capital and ecosystems on which we all depend, and reduce poverty and hunger. The key is strong agricultural research and extension systems. Research is important because agricultural activity is highly localized and requires adapted varieties and farming practices, and extension because the best research will be useless if it does not reach and become accepted by the millions of small farmers throughout the developing world.

But agricultural research is a very long-term enterprise. It takes about eight to twelve years of research to produce a new crop variety. Research cannot be turned on and off like a faucet: it requires continuity of funding. Unfortunately, with today's constrained budgets and prevailing attitudes toward aid in general, it is not always easy to get this sustained long-term commitment of donors to research objectives that would benefit the very poor in the world.

A spectacular success story in this area has been the impact on development of the Consultative Group on International Agricultural Research (CGIAR). The CGIAR is a voluntary association of donors supporting a research agenda focusing on international public-goods research, which is executed through seventeen international research centers. The CGIAR was largely responsible for the spread of new varieties of wheat, rice, and maize that, combined with the extension of irrigation and other factors, produced the "green revolution." The CGIAR represents a model of voluntary international cooperation for pursuing important research goals for humanity. It is apolitical, dedicated to excellence, and well focused on promoting sustainable agriculture for food security. It deals with the orphan crops that are of primary interest to the poor, not the cash crops that governments and the private sector have supported. It addresses the problems of agriculture in ecological zones where the poor tend to reside (tropical, semi-arid, arid, and mountain zones). The CGIAR has many success stories to its credit (see box 3-25).

To preserve the world's heritage of plant resources, the CGIAR has built *ex situ* collections of over 600,000 samples. CGIAR gene banks hold some 3,000 species of plants, of which more than 200 are major crops or forages. These collections are held in trust for humanity and are freely available to plant-breeders and other users throughout the world. Each year, over 120,000 samples from the in-trust collections and some 500,000 samples of improved materials are distributed, mostly in developing countries, for use by scientists, national agricultural research systems (NARS), and farmers. In addition, the CGIAR has sponsored the preservation of more than 150 species in the gene banks of some 450 non-CGIAR institutions.

We need to reinforce the CGIAR and build stronger links between it and NARS scientists and other actors involved in agricultural research in developing countries. We need to find other opportunities to build such cooperation.

Box 3-25. Consultative Group on International Agricultural Research

The CGIAR, established in 1971, is a voluntary association of 42 donors, with the World Bank, FAO, UNDP, and UNEP as cosponsors, supporting 16 international agricultural research centers dedicated to the promotion of sustainable agriculture for food security in developing countries. Productivity and natural resource management are twin pillars of research. Food crops, forestry, livestock, irrigation management, marine resources, and services to national agricultural research systems in developing countries are included in the research agenda of the CGIAR. Research covers commodities that provide 75 percent of food energy and a similar share of protein requirements in developing countries. Production in developing countries would be poorer by several 100 million tons a year of staple food without CGIAR-supported research.

Following are some highlights.

Wheat and rice. High-yielding wheat varieties developed at CGIAR centers are grown on over 50 million hectares of the 69 million hectares of wheat land in developing countries, including China. In the major rice-producing countries of Asia and Latin America, modern CGIAR-developed rice varieties are planted on between 80 and 100 percent of the total rice area.

Other crops. Steady progress has been made in the production of disease-resistant, high-yielding varieties of millet, sorghum, potato, sweet potato, forages, and livestock. Africa's cassava yields doubled in the past six years as a result of farmers adopting new varieties from CGIAR centers. Currently, cassava cultivars with an even higher yield potential are being tested by farmers. Over half the beans grown in Argentina, Costa Rica, Cuba, Guatemala, and Rwanda are derived from CGIAR varieties.

Crop protection. Integrated pest management programs and biological control methods are saving crops from destruction while enabling farmers to reduce the use of pesticides. For every dollar spent by the CGIAR's cassava mealybug biological control program in Africa, African farmers annually reap $149 in increased food productivity. In Asia, Indonesia has used pest-resistant rices drawn from cooperative research efforts as the foundation of a highly successful integrated pest management program that saves the country some $100 million annually in pesticide expenditures. Of the major food crops, potato requires the heaviest application of pesticides. The use of pesticides is reduced, however, by the development of a "hairy potato" plant resistant to a wide range of insect pests.

Institution building. The CGIAR has strengthened national research systems through consultation, research, and training. Over 45,000 developing-country scientists have received training in or through the CGIAR system from the CGIAR's inception through 1989 (the last year in which a survey was conducted).

Investment returns. A recent study on the impact of international agricultural research in Latin America showed that the $22.3 million spent in 1990 by the three Latin America–based CGIAR centers on beans, maize, rice, and wheat research returned over $1 billion a year to the region in terms of increased production, roughly forty-six times the research investment.

Environmentally Sustainable Development: Paradigm of the 1990s

Bringing together the various strands of the lessons learned in the last four decades of development theories and practical application, it is clear that "Sustainable Development" is the key phrase that captures the orientation of current and future efforts at promoting development.

For a first cut at an operational definition of sustainable development, we may begin with the Brundtland Commission's statement:

> Sustainable development is development that meets the needs of the present without compromising the ability of future generations to meet their own needs.[79]

The Brundtland Commission points out that this definition contains within it two concepts:

• Needs, in particular the essential needs of the world's poor, to which overriding priority should be given

• Limitations, imposed by the state of technology and social organization on the environment's ability to meet present needs.

To give special emphasis to the nonsocioeconomic aspects of development, the World Bank has added the environmental qualifier, to yield "environmentally sustainable development" (ESD). ESD was very much the theme of the 1992 Rio Earth Summit and has been one of the themes that governed the recent reorganization of the World Bank when as of January 1, 1993, this author was named vice president for environmentally sustainable development. The UN has also reorganized itself and created a Special Commission for Sustainable Development. Nitin Desai, deputy secretary-general for the UN Conference on Environment and Development (UNCED), has been named UN under-secretary general for policy coordination and sustainable development.

What does this slogan, "environmentally sustainable development," mean?

Figure 3-17. Objectives of Environmentally Sustainable Development

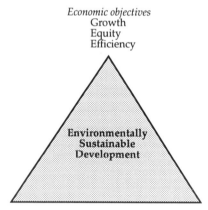

Economic objectives
Growth
Equity
Efficiency

Social objectives
Empowerment
Social mobility
Social cohesion
Cultural identity
Institutional development

Ecological objectives
Ecosystem integrity
Carrying capacity
Biodiversity
Global issues

It means introducing the concept of sustainability over the long term into the short-term analysis of development decisions and strategies. More important, it means bringing together the skills and concerns of different disciplines to address the multifaceted reality of the development challenge.[80] This multidisciplinary approach is captured in the diagram in figure 3-17, which sets out the economic, social, and ecological objectives.

For the *economic objective*, economists need to address the proper (and full) valuation of natural resources, the appropriate discount rate, the maintenance of capital stock, national income accounts, the promotion of growth with equity, poverty reduction, and, perhaps most important, the internalization of much that current economic models treat as "externalities."

For the *social objective*, sociologists, cultural anthropologists, political scientists, community organizers, and others need to address poverty in its societal, cultural, and structural context, as well as empowerment, the civic society, social mobility, and dynamics—all that goes into creating what Robert Putnam calls "social capital."[81] Neglect of this objective leads to the disintegration of societies, as we have been all too forcefully reminded by the recent tragedies in Somalia, Yugoslavia, and Zaire.

For the *ecological objective*, natural scientists and ecologists must bring to bear their arsenal of tools to address ecosystem integrity, carrying capacity, habitat conservation, and species interaction.

The ultimate challenge is to bring together the three objectives into a coherent whole.[82] Doing so will not be easy since the analytical frameworks of the different disciplines are different. But it must be done. Without the integrated perspective that ESD brings, the future of our species and this planet, not just of the poor among us, may be dim indeed.

Envoi

These key lessons learned from over four decades of experience with international development assistance show that the approaches of aid agencies are evolving as they learn the lessons of past experience.

Whether these new approaches will help surmount the many obstacles faced by developing countries remains to be seen. Clearly, however, the biggest challenge is likely to be Sub-Saharan Africa, where the case for effective assistance will be made or lost, for Africa is a region where success remains elusive, livelihoods precarious, and misery pervasive. Success there, as elsewhere, depends on tackling the difficult task of empowering people to take charge of their destinies. For progress, real progress, lies in empowering the poor, the weak, and the marginalized to become the producers of their own bounty and welfare, not the recipients of charity or the beneficiaries of aid.

4. Where Do We Go from Here?

In the final analysis the world we live in is changing very rapidly. Not only is the grip of the cold war finally relaxed, but the specter of nuclear holocaust is fast receding. Yet, the emerging new world order is tentative and fragile. Conflicts abound, and they are no less murderous for being local and confined.

Our appreciation of the interdependence among nations extends from the mutual benefits of expanded trade to the values of cultural exchange. Our vision of global interdependence is now extending to the very fabric of our ecosystem, encompassing all forms of life. Yet, we do not appear willing to extend this intellectual appreciation to a concept of *shared citizenship* to all the peoples of the earth.

Within the confines of the nation state, most people will accept that a minimum of equity and mutual solidarity is an essential ingredient of maintaining the fabric of society. However, once that imaginary line we call a frontier is crossed, the rules of behavior change. The gap between the rich and the poor has been diminished within many OECD countries, but it is growing on a global scale.

Although the developing countries have, on average, reasonably kept pace with the OECD countries in per capita income growth rates, the poorest developing countries have not fared as well. Indeed, the poorest 20 percent of humanity is falling further behind every decade, a point stressed at the beginning of this essay. Thus the richest 20 percent of the world's population went from being 30 times as rich as the poorest 20 percent in 1960 to being 60 times as rich in 1990. Many of these poor are in southern Asia and Sub-Saharan Africa and should be the prime targets of development assistance, both technical and financial.

This income disparity far exceeds anything witnessed within any one country. Figure 4-1 demonstrates this relationship.

In fact, this discrepancy is so vast that it needs to be compared to country situations to be fully appreciated. If one were to ask what amount of national income would have to be transferred to the poorest members of society to raise them all to the level of half the

Figure 4-1. Global Distribution of Income

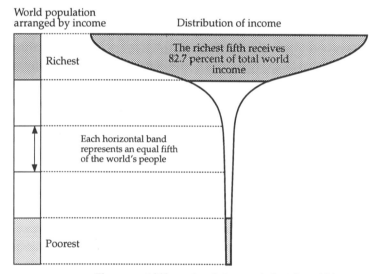

The poorest fifth receives 1.4 percent of total world income

Note: Global economic growth rarely filters down. The global income distribution by quintile is as follows:

World population	World income
Richest 20 percent	82.7 percent
Second 20 percent	11.7 percent
Third 20 percent	2.3 percent
Fourth 20 percent	1.9 percent
Poorest 20 percent	1.4 percent

Source: United Nations Development Programme, *Human Development Report 1992* (New York: Oxford University Press, 1992), inside front cover.

average income of the country, the answers would be along the following orders of magnitude:

Sweden	2.5 percent
United States	6.0 percent
Brazil	12.3 percent
World	25.0 percent

Against this backdrop, the commitment made by the rich countries to provide 0.7 percent of GNP in development assistance is not an overwhelming objective. The Nordic countries have exceeded that objective by a solid margin. Yet the aggregate OECD figure today stands at about 0.30 percent, largely because of the low figures appropriated by some of the larger donors.

But as I have argued throughout this essay, it is not just the amount of assistance that is at issue; it is much more *how* these funds are deployed and made available to the poorer countries—whether they are disbursed in a way that promotes a responsible partnership between donor and recipient and ensures that the aid reaches the intended beneficiaries. This distinction certainly does not mean more of the same old approaches to development assistance, especially not the politicized bilateral aid that was the norm for most assistance during the cold war. It means the adoption of the kind of approaches that have been sketched out in this essay to help those who help themselves to become the producers of their own welfare rather than the beneficiaries of aid.

Prospects for the Poor

What then are the prospects for the poor? Can they be expected to "close the gap" and catch up to the industrial societies of the North? Clearly not. This is an unrealistic target and one that would probably not be sustainable in terms of the environment. The planet cannot sustain its projected population, some 10 billion people, all consuming and polluting at the current OECD per capita levels. Of course, this argues as much for significant changes in the OECD patterns of consumption and pollution as it argues for a sounder development path for the developing countries.

What then are the prospects for this poorest 20 to 25 percent of humanity? Luckily, they do not have to attain the per capita income levels of the North to very significantly improve their well-being.

Figure 4-2 shows the correlation between per capita income and life expectancy at birth, probably the best single indicator of well-being. As expected, it is positively correlated: the richer one is, the longer one lives. But the relationship is not linear. In fact, at about $1,500 per capita, life expectancy levels are equal to about 80 percent or more of those enjoyed at per capita incomes of $20,000. This same pattern is found to hold for other social indicators as well. Furthermore, the family of curves shown in figure 4-2 indicates that for the same per capita income level, we can now obtain considerably better social results because of, among other measures, sounder nutrition policies and greater attention to preventive medicine.

Achieving per capita income levels in the $1,500 to $2,000 range,

Figure 4–2. Life expectancy versus Per Capita GNP, Best Fit Relation by Decade

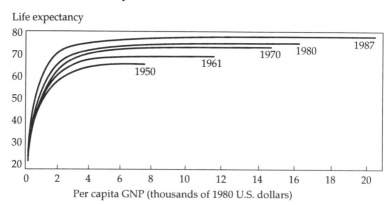

Source: Gregory K. Ingram, "Economic Development: Its Record and Determinants," in *CIOS XXI World Management Congress: Management Challenges for the 1990s; Program and Plenary Proceedings* (New York: North American Management Council, 1990).

coupled with sound social, economic, and environmental policies within a reasonable time frame, is a realistic objective. It should govern much of the development assistance strategies in the 1990s. Achieving this objective will require that the countries of the South undertake major internal reform of their macroeconomic policies and focus on the priorities of human resources and the creation of an enabling environment, both politically and economically, to allow individuals and groups to flourish. International assistance should be directed to supporting such policies and to nurturing the creation of ever-greater national capacities.

Although total external financial flows are not likely to be more than a small part of the total financing needs of poor countries, they can be quite effective if they are well focused, timely, and provided in a supportive fashion. This is the challenge for development assistance in the 1990s: to establish an effective *partnership* between the rich and the poor in support of the poor's efforts to promote sustainable development.

A Vision of Development in the 1990s

Let me close with a vision. A vision of development as we approach the third millennium. A vision that sees development like a tree, which is nurtured by feeding its roots, not by pulling on its branches. We must empower people to be all they can be—to create their own identities, their own institutions.

This is a vision of sustainable development that is people-centered and gender-conscious, and that seeks equity for all and empowerment of the weak and the vulnerable everywhere that they may be the producers of their own welfare and bounty, not the recipients of charity or beneficiaries of aid.

A vision that has no room for complacency in the face of the misery of millions of kindred souls who suffer in the grip of extreme poverty and hunger in a world that has the means and the ability to help them lift themselves out of conditions that are beneath any definition of human decency.

A vision that considers the need to abolish such conditions as a simple expression of respect for the most basic of human rights, and that considers the failure to strive for the elimination of the scourge of hunger as a degrading complicity in an unacceptable state of affairs.

A vision that recognizes that development must have a cultural content, recognizes that governance and institution building and enhancing human capacities are all central parts of the development process and may in fact be the keys that undergird economic well-being.

It is a vision that places short-term actions within a long-term framework. It is a vision of development that is environmentally sustainable, recognizes the interdependence of all living things, leads us to act in ways that will leave the future generations as much as if not more than what we found ourselves, and will husband the resources of this fragile planet just as we learn to use its bounty.

This vision is not a denial of the importance of economic management and growth but is a recognition that economic growth is only one part of development.

How can we reconcile that vision with the hard calculus of economics and finance? On one level, human beings are no more than three buckets of water and a handful of minerals held together by chemical reactions. This reductionist view has served us well in medicine and science and enabled us to produce major improvements in human well-being. But it is a partial image, one that misses the difference between a Hitler and a Mother Teresa, one that misses the difference between a Stalin and a Mozart. It misses all those special features that make human beings human.

In the same spirit, reducing a society to the sum of its economic and financial transactions is the equivalent of reducing this society to three buckets of water and a handful of minerals. It misses all those marvelous, amazing things that human beings create through their interactions with other human beings and with their environment—all that we have learned to call a human society, a community, a sense of place, a culture.

We have the opportunity to change the way humanity relates to its environment. It is a challenge that we, at the World Bank, are determined to meet—working collaboratively with our partners who share this objective. We cannot afford to let this opportunity escape us, either by sins of commission or of omission. We can think of better ways of promoting development, we can convince policy-makers and the world at large.

It can be done. It must be done. It will be done.

Notes

1. This section draws upon "Our Common Humanity: The Crisis of Values in Contemporary Society," *EAIE Newsletter* 13 (February 1994): 3–10 (keynote address to the Fifth Annual Conference of the European Association for International Education, The Hague, December 2, 1993).

2. Francis Fukuyama, *The End of History and the Last Man* (New York: The Free Press, 1992).

3. Robert Putnam, with Robert Leonardi and Raffaella Nanetti, *Making Democracy Work: Civic Traditions in Modern Italy* (Princeton: Princeton University Press, 1993).

4. Ismail Serageldin, "Mirrors and Windows," parts I and II, *Litterae, Review of the European Academy of Sciences and Arts* 3(2–3) (1993): 4–15, and 4(1)(1994): 8–26. Also appeared in *American Journal of Islamic Social Studies* 11(Spring 1994): 79–107.

5. United Nations, *Human Rights: A Compilation of International Instruments*, vol. 1, *Universal Instruments* (New York, 1993).

6. For a recent review of the subject, see, among others, Mark J. Miller, ed., "Strategies for Immigration Control: An International Comparison," *American Academy of Political and Social Science*, vol. 534 (July 1994). See especially the essays by Gary P. Freeman, "Can Liberal States Control Unwanted Migration?" (17–30), and W. Roger Böhning, "Helping Migrants to Stay at Home" (165–77).

7. UNESCO, 1990.

8. See George Gilder's excellent essay, "The Death of Telephony," in *The Economist* 328 (September 11, 1993): 75–78.

9. For a historical survey of development assistance, see Rutherford Poats, *Twenty-Five Years of Development Cooperation—A Review: Efforts and Policies of the Members of the Development Assistance Committee* (Paris: Organization for Economic Cooperation and Development, 1985).

10. Debt Reporting System, World Bank, Washington, D.C. DAC members include Australia, Austria, Canada, the European Economic Community, Finland, Japan, New Zealand, Norway, Sweden, Switzerland, and the United States.

11. Organization for Economic Cooperation and Development and

Development Assistance Committee, *Development Cooperation: Efforts and Policies of the Members of the Development Assistance Committee, 1991 Report* (Paris: 1991), 126.

12. Organization for Economic Cooperation and Development and Development Assistance Committee, *Development Cooperation*, 125. For more details on aid flows, see Joseph C. Wheeler, *Development Cooperation in the 1990s: Efforts and Policies of the Members of the Development Assistance Committee, 1989 Report* (Paris: Organization for Economic Cooperation and Development, 1989); and Joseph Wheeler, "The Critical Role for Official Development Assistance in the 1990s," *Finance & Development* 26 (September 1989): 38–40.

13. For a review of the literature, see Jonathan Eaton, "Foreign Capital Flows," in *Handbook of Development Economics*, ed. Hollis Chenery and T. N. Srinivasan, vol. 2 (New York: North Holland, 1989). The World Bank's *World Development Report 1991: The Challenge of Development* (New York: Oxford University Press, 1991) provides an excellent summary of the advantages and disadvantages of aid.

14. This can also be explained in a more formal setting in which aid is derived from the maximization of a social welfare function. See Eaton, "Foreign Capital Flows."

15. For a review of these various studies, see K. Jay and C. Michalopoulos, "Donor Policies, Donor Interests, and Aid Effectiveness," in *Aid and Development*, ed. Anne O. Krueger and Constantine Michalopoulos (Baltimore: Johns Hopkins University Press, 1989).

16. Eaton, "Foreign Capital Flows."

17. For a summary of Bauer's views, see Gerald Meier and Dudley Seers, eds., *Pioneers in Development*, 2d ser. (New York: Oxford University Press, 1987).

18. P. T. Bauer and Basil Yamey, "Foreign Aid: What Is at Stake?" *The Public Interest* 68 (Summer 1982): 55.

19. The presence of children under six and over eleven years old in the primary schools, the latter of whom usually repeated grades, accounts for a percentage greater than 100.

20. See, for example, Anne O. Krueger and Vernon Ruttan, "The Development of Economic Assistance to LDCs" (University of Minnesota, Economic Development Center, for the United States Agency for International Development and the Department of State, 1983); Anne O. Krueger, "Aid in the Development Process," *World Bank Research Observer* 1 (January 1986): 57–78; and Krueger and Michalopoulos, eds., *Aid and Development*.

21. Robert Cassen and others, *Does Aid Work? Report on an Intergovernmental Task Force* (Oxford: Clarendon Press, 1987).

22. Krueger and Michalopoulos, *Aid and Development.*

23. Paul Mosley and others, "Aid, the Public Sector and the Market in LDCs," *Economic Journal* 97 (September 1987): 616–41.

24. Cassen reports the average rate of return of projects funded by the World Bank as 17 percent. Cassen and others, *Does Aid Work?*

25. Lawrence H. Summers, *The Challenge of Development: Some Lessons of History for Sub-Saharan Africa,* Nigerian Institute of International Affairs Lecture Series no. 74 (Lagos: Nigerian Institute of International Affairs, 1992).

26. Bauer and Yamey, "Foreign Aid: What Is at Stake?" 61.

27. World Bank, *Sub-Saharan Africa: From Crisis to Sustainable Growth;* (Washington, D.C., 1989).

28. See, among others, Ismail Serageldin, "Governance, Democracy and the World Bank in Africa" (Paper, Office of the Vice President, Environmentally Sustainable Development, World Bank, Washington, D.C., September 20, 1990); Pierre Landell-Mills and Ismail Serageldin, "Governance and the External Factor," in *Proceedings of the World Bank Annual Conference on Development Economics 1991,* ed. Lawrence H. Summers and Shekhar Shah (Washington, D.C.: World Bank, 1992), 303–20; and Pierre Landell-Mills and Ismail Serageldin, "Governance and the Development Process," *Finance & Development* 28 (September 1991): 14–17; and Pierre Landell-Mills, "Governance, Cultural Change, and Empowerment," *Journal of Modern African Studies* 30 (3) (1992): 543–67.

29. Cassen and others, *Does Aid Work?*

30. See Landell-Mills and Serageldin, "Governance and the External Factor"; and Joan M. Nelson, with Stephanie J. Eglinton, *Encouraging Democracy: What Role for Conditioned Aid?* Policy Essay 4 (Washington, D.C.: Overseas Development Council, 1992).

31. Landell-Mills, "Governance, Cultural Change, and Empowerment."

32. "If protection levels in the EC, the United States, and Japan were to be reduced by 50 percent, developing countries could increase exports by 15 percent, or US$50 billion in 1988 prices. . . . This amounts to US$54 billion in 1991 prices, almost equivalent to the aggregate net resource flows from official sources to developing countries in 1991." World Bank, *Global Economic Prospects and the Developing Countries 1992* (Washington, D.C. 1992), 20–22.

33. For a review of evaluation methods of aid programs, see Basil Cracknell, "Evaluating Development Assistance: A Review of the Literature," *Public Administration and Development* 8 (January–March 1988): 75–83.

34. Cassen and others, *Does Aid Work?*

35. See Ismail Serageldin, *Development Partners: Aid and Cooperation in*

the 1990s (Stockholm: Swedish International Development Authority, 1993).

36. "Development and International Economic Cooperation: An Agenda for Development," Report of the Secretary General of the United Nations, May 6, 1994.

37. See United Nations Development Programme, *Human Development Report* for the years 1990, 1991, and 1992 (New York: Oxford University Press).

38. This section is drawn from Ismail Serageldin, Adewale Sangowawa, and Ahmedou Ould-Abdallah, with Sadek Wahba and Maria Cristina Germany, "African Development: Diagnosis and Recommendations," in Olusegun Obasanjo and Felix G. N. Mosha, eds., *Africa: Rise to Challenge—Towards a Conference on Security, Stability, Development and Cooperation in Africa* (Abeokuta, Nigeria: Africa Leadership Forum, 1993).

39. World Bank, *World Development Report 1992: Development and the Environment* (New York: Oxford University Press, 1992).

40. For the basic arguments underlying the empowerment of women and gender-responsive development, see Caroline O. N. Moser, "Gender Planning in the Third World: Meeting Practical and Strategic Gender Needs," *World Development* 17 (11) (1989): 1799–825. See also Ingrid Palmer, "Gender and Population in the Adjustment of African Economies: Planning for Change," *Women, Work and Development Series*, no. 19 (Geneva: International Labour Office, 1991). For the last twenty years, since the beginning of the United Nations Decade of Women in 1975, UN member countries and bilateral and multilateral donors have made increasingly serious efforts, to "mainstream" women in the development process and related assistance strategies. For an explanation and report on these efforts see "Mainstreaming Women in Development in Different Settings," Report for OECD/DAC/WID Expert Group (Paris, 1992).

41. See Amartya K. Sen, "Women's Survival as a Development Problem" (Comments prepared for the 1700th Stated Meeting of the American Academy of Arts and Sciences, March 8, 1989); and Amartya K. Sen, "More than 100 Million Women Are Missing," *New York Review of Books* 37 (December 20, 1990): 61–66.

42. Lawrence H. Summers, *Investing in All the People*, Policy Research Working Paper WPS 905 (Washington, D.C.: Office of the Vice President and Chief Economist, World Bank, 1992), 6.

43. Dennis de Tray, "Child Quality and the Demand for Children," *Journal of Political Economy* (March–April 1973): S70–95; reprinted in T. W. Schultz, ed., *Economics of the Family* (Chicago: University of Chicago

Press, 1974), and in Rand Corporation, P-4848, July 1972. This order of magnitude is confirmed for Kenya in Marcia Schafgans, "Household Allocations in Kenya" (Paper, Women in Development Division, Population and Human Resources Department, World Bank, Washington, D.C., August 1991); for urban dwellers in Peru in Barbara K. Herz and Shahidur R. Khandker, eds., *Women's Work, Education, and Family Welfare in Peru*, World Bank Discussion Paper 116 (Washington, D.C.: World Bank, 1991); and for Thailand in T. Paul Schultz, "The Relationship between Local Family Planning Expenditures and Fertility in Thailand, 1976–81" (Center Discussion Paper no. 662, Economic Growth Center, Yale University, New Haven, Conn., April 1992).

44. Summers, *Investing in All the People*, 9.

45. Raymond Gastil, *Freedom in the World* (New York: Freedom House, 1989), cited in World Bank, *World Development Report 1991: The Challenge of Development* (New York: Oxford University Press, 1991), 50.

46. Charles Humana's human freedom index, cited in United Nations Development Programme, *Human Development Report 1991*, 19–21.

47. See Ibrahim F. I. Shihata, "The World Bank and 'Governance' Issues in Its Borrowing Members," chap. 2 in Franziska Tschofen and Antonio R. Parra, comp. and ed., *The World Bank in a Changing World: Selected Essays* (Dordrecht, the Netherlands: Martinus Nijhoff Publishers, 1991).

48. Transparency International was launched as an international NGO in May 1993. An interim board has been established under the chairmanship of Dr. Peter Eigen of GTZ in Berlin.

49. This distinguished international NGO was awarded the Nobel Peace Prize in 1977.

50. See the pioneering work of Putnam, with Leonardi and Nanetti, *Making Democracy Work*.

51. See E. F. Schumacher, *Small Is Beautiful* (New York: Perennial Library, 1989).

52. See John Clark, *Democratizing Development: The Role of Voluntary Organizations* (West Hartford, Conn.: Kumarian Press, 1991).

53. See *The Enabling Environment Conference: Effective Private Sector Contribution to Development in Sub-Saharan Africa—The Nairobi Statement* (Geneva: Aga Khan Foundation, 1987).

54. See World Bank, *World Development Report 1983* (New York: Oxford University Press, 1983).

55. See World Bank, *African Capacity Building Initiative: Toward Improved Policy Analysis and Development Management* (Washington, D.C.: World Bank, 1990).

56. Sunita Kikeri, John Nellis, and Mary Shirley, *Privatization: The*

Lessons of Experience (Washington, D.C.: World Bank, 1992), 21.

57. Kikeri, Nellis, and Shirley, *Privatization*, 30.

58. World Bank, *Toward Sustained Development: A Joint Program of Action for Sub-Saharan Africa*, Report PUB 5228, 2 vols. (Washington, D.C. 1984).

59. In 1966 when he was U.S. secretary of defense, Robert McNamara made the case that security would be better served by investing in development than by investing in bombs. He first established statistically the *"irrefutable relationship between violence and economic backwardness"*: the overwhelming majority of violent internal conflicts are in poorer countries—thirty-two of the thirty-eight very poor nations experienced significant major outbreaks of violence between 1958 and 1966, compared with only one of the twenty-seven rich nations. He then stated, "In a modernizing society, *security means development*. Security is *not* military hardware—though it may include it. Security is *not* military force—though it may involve it. . . . Security *is* development. *Without* development, there can be no security. . . . Security . . . implies a minimal measure of order and stability. Without internal development . . . order and stability are simply not possible . . . because human nature cannot be frustrated beyond intrinsic limits" [emphasis in the original]. Robert S. McNamara (Address before the American Society of Newspaper Editors, Montreal, May 18, 1966; World Bank, Washington, D.C.), 4, 8.

60. Particularly noteworthy is the work of Ruth Leger Sivard, who has published annually a review of military and social expenditures highlighting these issues. See, for example, Ruth Leger Sivard, *World Military and Social Expenditures 1991*, 14th ed. (Washington, D.C.: World Priorities, 1991).

61. Barber B. Conable (Address to the Board of Governors of the World Bank Group, External Affairs Department, World Bank, Washington, D.C., September 26, 1989).

62. A legal opinion on the statutory limits of World Bank involvement in matters of military spending was given by the Bank's vice president and general counsel on December 13, 1991. It argued that the Bank should look at military spending, in the context of overall government spending, focusing on protecting development spending rather than addressing what an appropriate level of military spending should be.

63. Ismail Serageldin, "Military Spending in Developing Countries," *Bank's World* 9 (6) (June 1990): 10–11.

64. See Robert S. McNamara, "Military Expenditure and Development," 95–125; Mary Kaldor, "After the Cold War: Obstacles and Opportunities in Cutting Arms Budgets," 141–56; and Saadet Deger and Somnath Sen, "Military Expenditure, Aid, and Economic

Development," 159–89, all in *Proceedings of the World Bank Annual Conference on Development Economics 1991* (Washington, D.C.: World Bank, 1992).

65. McNamara, "Military Expenditure and Development," 107.

66. Global Coalition for Africa, "Reducing Military Expenditure in Africa," Document GCA/AC.2/04/4/92 (Report presented at the Second Advisory Committee Meeting of the Global Coalition for Africa, Kampala, Uganda, May 8–9, 1992; Global Coalition for Africa, Washington, D.C.); Nicole Ball, *Pressing for Peace: Can Aid Induce Reform?* Policy Essay no. 6 (Washington, D.C.: Overseas Development Council, 1992); and Nicole Ball, "Options for DAC Members on Linking Military Expenditures and Aid" (Discussion Paper for the Workshop on Military Expenditure and Aid, Ministry of Foreign Affairs, Tokyo, November 6, 1992). See also Takao Kawakami, "Japan's ODA Policies for a Peace Initiative" (Address before the Tokyo Conference on Arms Reduction and Economic Development in the Post–Cold War Era, Tokyo, November 5, 1992).

67. Shankar N. Acharya and Sanjay Pradhan, "Economic Consequences of War/Peace Transitions in Africa: Choices for Public Finance" (Study underway, Public Economics Division, Country Economics Department, World Bank, Washington, D.C.); and Sarah Keener, Suzanne Heigh, Luiz Pereira da Silva, and Nicole Ball, "Demobilization and Reintegration of Military Personnel in Africa: The Evidence from Seven Country Case Studies," Africa Regional Series Report no. IDP–130, World Bank, Washington, D.C., October 1993. See also Herbert M. Howe, "National Reconciliation and a New South African Defense Force" (Address before the Institute on African Affairs at the 1992 Conference on African Policy Issues, Washington, D.C., April 23, 1992); and Herbert M. Howe, "Military Integration in Zimbabwe, 1980" (Address before the African Studies Association, Seattle, Wash., November 20, 1992) (both are available from the Office of the Director of African Studies, School of Foreign Service, Georgetown University, Washington, D.C.).

68. Anthony Lake and contributors, *After the Wars: Reconstruction in Afghanistan, Indochina, Central America, Southern Africa, and the Horn of Africa*, U.S.–Third World Policy Perspectives 16 (Washington, D.C.: Overseas Development Council, 1990).

69. Amartya K. Sen, "Values, Capability and Well-Being in Development Assistance" (Paper presented to the SIDA Workshop on Development Assistance from the Perspective of Recipient Countries, Stockholm, April 26–28, 1989); and Amartya K. Sen, "International Freedom as a Social Commitment," *New York Review of Books* 37 (June 14, 1990): 49–55.

NOTES

NOTES

70. See, among others, J. Roland Pennock, "Rights, Natural Rights, and Human Rights: A General View," in J. Roland Pennock and John W. Chapman, eds., *Human Rights: Nomos XXIII*, (New York: New York University, 1981), 1–28.

71. For a general discussion of human rights and the World Bank, see Shihata, "The World Bank and 'Governance' Issues."

72. Jean Dreze and Amartya K. Sen, *Hunger and Public Action* (Oxford: Clarendon Press, 1989); Jean Dreze and Amartya K. Sen, eds., *The Political Economy of Hunger*, 3 vols. (Oxford: Clarendon Press, 1990); and Jean Dreze, Amartya K. Sen, and Suntory-Toyota International Centre for Economics and Related Disciplines, *Public Action for Social Security: Foundations and Strategy*, DEP Series no. 20 (London: Development Economics Research Programme and Suntory-Toyota International Centre for Economics and Related Disciplines, 1989).

73. *Webster's New Collegiate Dictionary* (Springfield, Mass.: Merriam-Webster, Inc., 1975), 1112.

74. The most important of these are the Universal Declaration of Human Rights, adopted and proclaimed by UN General Assembly Resolution 217 (III), December 10, 1948; the International Covenant on Economic, Social and Cultural Rights, adopted and opened for signature, ratification, and accession by UN General Assembly Resolution 2200 A (XI), December 16, 1966, 21 UN GAO Supp. (No. 16), at 49, UN Doc. A/6316 (1967), which took effect on January 3, 1976; and the International Covenant on Civil and Political Rights, adopted and opened for signature, ratification, and accession by General Assembly Resolution 2200 A (XI), December 16, 1966, 21 UN GAO Supp. (No. 16), at 49, UN Doc. A/6316 (1967), which took effect on March 23, 1976. Cited in Ibrahim F. I. Shihata, "The World Bank and Human Rights," chap. 3 in *The World Bank in a Changing World: Selected Essays*. There are other instruments as well. See Division of Human Rights, United Nations, *Human Rights: A Compilation of International Instruments* (New York: United Nations, 1978 and following years).

75. For discussion of the UN General Assembly resolutions, see Shihata, "World Bank and Human Rights," especially 99–109.

76. Some scholars argue that since sovereignty means state jurisdiction within the limits defined by international law, what is being discussed here is the evolving modern definition of these limits, not a breaching of a fixed and unchangeable concept.

77. The UN Declaration of Human Rights is in a different category from the treaties. Although initially it was not technically binding, some legal scholars argue that it is now part of customary universal law and that it prevails over treaties.

78. World Bank, "Resettlement and Development: The Bankwide Review of Projects Involving Involuntary Resettlement, 1986–1993," Environment Department, Washington, D.C., 1994.

79. Brundtland Commission (World Commission on Environment and Development), *Our Common Future* (New York: Oxford University Press, 1987), 43.

80. See Ismail Serageldin, "Making Development Sustainable," *Finance & Development* 30 (December 1993): 6–10.

81. See Robert D. Putnam, "Social Capital and Public Affairs," *American Prospect* 13 (Spring 1993): 1–8.

82. See Ismail Serageldin and Andrew Steer, eds., *Making Development Sustainable: From Concepts to Action* (Washington, D.C.: World Bank, 1994).

Bibliography

Acharya, Shankar, and Sanjay Pradhan. "Economic Consequences of War/Peace Transitions in Africa: Choices for Public Finance." Study. Public Economics Division, Country Economics Department, World Bank, Washington, D.C. Forthcoming.

Africa Leadership Forum. "The Conventions on SSDCA 1991." In *The Kampala Document: Towards a Conference on Security, Stability, Development and Cooperation in Africa.* Kampala, Uganda, May 19–22, 1991. Abeokuta, Nigeria: Africa Leadership Forum, 1991.

Africa Technical Department. "Zambia: Financial Performance of the Government-Owned Transport Sector." Report. Africa Technical Department for the Southern Africa Department, World Bank, August 26, 1992.

African Development Bank, United Nations Development Programme, and the World Bank. *The Social Dimensions of Adjustment in Africa: A Policy Agenda.* Washington, D.C.: World Bank, 1990.

African Heads of State and Government. Resolution AHG/Res. 8 (XXVI). Summit meeting at Addis Ababa, June 11, 1990.

Aga Khan Foundation, *The Enabling Environment Conference: Effective Private Sector Contribution to Development in Sub-Saharan Africa—The Nairobi Statement.* Geneva, 1987.

Ahmed, Masood, and Lawrence H. Summers. "A Tenth Anniversary Report on the Debt Crisis." *Finance & Development* 29 (3) (September 1992): 2–5.

Ainsworth, Martha, and Mead Over. "The Economic Impact of AIDS: Shocks, Responses, and Outcomes." Population, Health and Nutrition Technical Working Paper no. 1. Washington, D.C.: Africa Technical Department, World Bank, 1992.

Ainsworth, Martha, and A.A. Rwegarulira. "Coping with the AIDS Epidemic in Tanzania: Survivor Assistance." Population, Health and Nutrition Technical Working Paper no. 6. Washington, D.C.: Africa Technical Department, World Bank, 1992.

Ball, Nicole. "Options for DAC Members on Linking Military Expenditures and Aid." Discussion Paper for the Workshop on Military Expenditure and Aid. Ministry of Foreign Affairs, Tokyo, November 6, 1992.

————. *Pressing for Peace: Can Aid Induce Reform?* Policy Essay no. 6. Washington, D.C.: Overseas Development Council, 1992.

————. "Reducing Military Expenditure in Africa." Paper prepared for the Global Coalition for Africa, Washington, D.C., March 31, 1992.

Barry, A. J. *Aid Co-ordination and Aid Effectiveness: A Review of Country and Regional Experience.* Paris: Organization for Economic Cooperation and Development, 1988.

Bauer, P. T. "Creating the Third World: Foreign Aid and Its Offspring." *Journal of Economic Growth* 2 (4) (1987): 3–9.

Bauer, P. T., and Basil Yamey. "Foreign Aid: What Is at Stake?" *The Public Interest,* 68 (Summer 1982): 53–69.

Baum, Warren C. "Project Cycle." *Finance & Development* 7 (2) (June 1970): 2–13.

————. "World Bank Project Cycle." *Finance & Development* 15 (4) (December 1978): 10–17.

————. *The Project Cycle.* Rev. ed. Washington, D.C.: World Bank, 1982.

Baum, Warren C., and Stokes M. Tolbert. *Investing in Development: Lessons of World Bank Experience.* New York: Oxford University Press, 1985.

Bayart, Jean-François. *L'Etat en Afrique: La politique du ventre.* Paris: Fayard, 1989.

Berg, Eliott J. *Rethinking Technical Cooperation: Reforms for Capacity Building in Africa.* New York: United Nations Development Programme, 1993.

Biggs, T. and B. Levy. "Strategic Interventions and the Political Economy of Industrial Policy in Developing Countries." In *Reforming Economic Systems in Developing Countries,* edited by Dwight H. Perkins and Michael Roemer. Cambridge: Harvard Institute for International Development, Harvard University, 1991.

Binswanger, Hans P., and Pierre Landell-Mills. *The World Bank's Strategy for Reducing Poverty and Hunger: A Report to the Development Community.* Environmentally Sustainable Development Studies and Monographs Series no. 4. Washington, D.C.: World Bank, 1995.

Boateng, E. Oti, and others. *A Poverty Profile for Ghana, 1987–88.* SDA Working Paper no. 5. Washington, D.C.: World Bank, 1990.

Böhning, W. Roger. "Helping Migrants to Stay at Home." In "Strategies for Immigration Control: An International Comparison," edited by Mark J. Miller. *Annals of the American Academy of Political and Social Science* 534(July 1994): 165–77.

Bos, Eduard, and Rodolfo A. Bulatao. "The Demographic Impact of AIDS in Sub-Saharan Africa: Short- and Long-Term Projections." Washington, D.C.: World Bank, 1992.

Bos, Eduard, My T. Vu, and Ann Levin. "East Asia and Pacific Region/South Asia Region Population Projections, 1992–93." Policy

Research Working Paper no. 1032. Washington, D.C.: World Bank, 1992.

Boutros-Ghali, Boutros. *An Agenda for Peace*. New York: United Nations, 1992.

Bradley, David, and others. *A Review of Environmental Health Impacts in Developing Country Cities*. Urban Management Program Discussion Paper no. 6. Washington, D.C.: World Bank, 1992.

Branigin, William. "The UN Empire." Series of four articles. *Washington Post*, September 20–23, 1992.

Brundtland Commission (World Commission on Environment and Development). *Our Common Future*. New York: Oxford University Press, 1987.

Buyck, Beatrice. "The Bank's Use of Technical Assistance for Institutional Development." Policy, Research, and External Affairs Working Paper WPS 578. Washington, D.C.: Country Economics Department, World Bank, 1991.

Cassen, Robert. "Effectiveness of Aid." *Finance & Development* 23 (1) (March 1986): 11–14.

Cassen, Robert, and others. *Does Aid Work? Report on an Intergovernmental Task Force*. Oxford: Clarendon Press, 1987.

Center for Defense Information data. Washington, D.C., March 1993.

Cernea, Michael M., and April Adams. *Sociology, Anthropology, and Development: An Annotated Bibliography of World Bank Publications 1975-1993*. Environmentally Sustainable Development Studies and Monographs Series no. 3. Washington, D.C.: World Bank, 1994.

Cernea, Michael M., ed. *Putting People First: Sociological Variables in Rural Development*, 2nd ed. New York: Oxford University Press, 1991.

Chabal, Patrick. *Political Domination in Africa*. Cambridge and New York: Cambridge University Press, 1986.

Chahnazarian, Anouch. "Determinants of the Sex Ratio at Birth (Hepatitis B)." Ph.D. diss., Princeton University, Princeton, N.J., 1986.

Chand, Sheetal, and Reinold van Til. "Ghana: Toward Successful Stabilization and Recovery." *Finance & Development* 25 (1) (March 1988): 32–35.

Chenery, Hollis, and Michael Bruno. "Development Alternatives in an Open Economy." *Economic Journal* 72 (March 1962): 79–103.

Chérif, M'hamed, and Ismail Serageldin. "Scénarios pour l'Afrique de l'an 2000." *Jeune Afrique* 1598–99 (August 14–27, 1991), 36–40.

Chhibber, Ajay, and Stanley Fischer, eds. *Economic Reform in Sub-Saharan Africa*. A World Bank Symposium. Washington, D.C.: World Bank, 1992.

Christoffersen, Leif, François Falloux, and Lee Talbot. "National Environmental Action Plans: First Lessons and Future Directions." Washington, D.C.: World Bank, 1990.

Clark, John. *Democratizing Development: The Role of Voluntary Organi-

zations. West Hartford, Conn.: Kumarian Press, 1991.

Cleaver, Kevin, and Götz A. Schreiber. *Reversing the Spiral: The Population, Agriculture, and Environment Nexus in Sub-Saharan Africa.* Washington, D.C.: World Bank, 1994.

Cleaver, Kevin, and others, eds. *Conservation of West and Central African Rainforests/Conservation de la forêt dense en Afrique centrale et de l'Ouest.* World Bank Environment Paper no. 1. Washington, D.C.: World Bank, in cooperation with IUCN—The World Conservation Union, 1992.

Cline, William. "Managing International Debt: How One Big Battle Was Won." *The Economist* 334(7902) (February 18-24, 1995): 17-19.

Club of Dublin. "National Environmental Action Plans in Africa." In Proceedings of a Workshop Organized by the Government of Ireland, the Environmental Institute, University College, Dublin, and the World Bank (EDIAR and AFTEN), Dublin, Ireland, December 12–14, 1990. Washington, D.C.: Environment Division, Africa Technical Department, World Bank, 1990.

———. "Issues Facing National Environmental Action Plans in Africa." In Report from a Club of Dublin Workshop, Mauritius, June 17–19, 1991. Washington, D.C.: Environment Division, Africa Technical Department, World Bank, 1991.

Coale, Ansley. "Excess Female Mortality and the Balance of the Sexes in the Population: An Estimate of the Number of 'Missing Females.'" *Population and Development Review* 17 (3) (September 1991): 517–23.

Colletta, Nat J., and Nicole Ball. "War to Peace Transition in Uganda." *Finance & Development* 30 (2) (June 1993): 36–39.

Conable, Barber. *Address to the Board of Governors of the World Bank Group;* World Bank, Washington, D.C., *September 26, 1989.*

Country Economics Department, World Bank. *The Reform of Public Sector Management: Lessons from Experience.* Policy and Research Series 18. Washington, D.C.: World Bank, 1991.

———. *Adjustment Lending and Mobilization of Private and Public Resources for Growth.* Policy and Research Series 22. Washington, D.C.: World Bank, 1992.

Cracknell, Basil. "Evaluating Development Assistance: A Review of the Literature." *Public Administration and Development* 8 (1) (January–March 1988): 75–83.

Crafts, N. C. R. "The Eighteenth Century: A Survey." In *The Economic History of Britain since 1700,* edited by Roderick Floud and Donald McCloskey. Cambridge: Cambridge University Press, 1981.

Culagovski, Jorge, Victor Gabor, Maria Cristina Germany, and Charles P. Humphreys. "African Financing Needs in the 1990s." Policy, Research, and External Affairs Working Paper WPS 764. Washington, D.C.:

Africa Technical Department, World Bank, 1991.

Dasgupta, Partha. *An Inquiry into Well-Being and Destitution.* Oxford: Clarendon Press; New York: Oxford University Press, 1993.

Deger, Saadet, and Somnath Sen. "Military Expenditure, Aid, and Economic Development." In *Proceedings of the World Bank Annual Conference on Development Economics 1991,* 159–89. Washington, D.C.: World Bank, 1992.

De Merode, Louis. "Civil Service Pay and Employment Reform in Africa: Selected Implementation Experiences." AFTIM Division Study Paper no. 2. Africa Technical Department, World Bank, Washington, D.C., 1991.

Deng, Lual, Markus Kostner, and Crawford Young, eds. *Democratization and Structural Adjustment in Africa in the 1990s.* Madison, Wis.: African Studies Program, University of Wisconsin, Madison, 1991.

De Soto, Hernan. *The Other Path.* New York: Harper & Row, 1989.

Dessing, Maryke. *Support for Microenterprises: Lessons for Sub-Saharan Africa.* World Bank Technical Paper no. 122. Washington, D.C.: World Bank, 1990.

De Tray, Dennis. "Child Quality and the Demand for Children." *Journal of Political Economy* (March–April 1973): S70-95. (Reprinted in Schultz, T. W., ed., *Economics of the Family,* Chicago: University of Chicago Press, 1974; also The Rand Corporation, P-4848, July 1972.)

Division of Human Rights, United Nations. *Human Rights: A Compilation of International Instruments.* New York: United Nations, 1978 *et seq.*

Dreze, Jean, and Amartya K. Sen. *Hunger and Public Action.* Oxford: Clarendon Press, 1989.

———, eds. *The Political Economy of Hunger.* 3 vols. Oxford: Clarendon Press, 1990.

Dreze, Jean, Amartya K. Sen, and Suntory-Toyota International Centre for Economics and Related Disciplines. *Public Action for Social Security: Foundations and Strategy.* DEP Series no. 20. London: Development Economics Research Programme and Suntory-Toyota International Centre for Economics and Related Disciplines, 1989.

Dubois, Jean-Luc, and Alexandre Marc. "Des p'tits boulots pour sortir de la crise." *Croissance: Le monde en développement,* no. 352 (September 1992): 30–37.

Eaton, Jonathan. "Foreign Capital Flows." In Hollis Chenery and T. N. Srinivasan, eds., *Handbook of Development Economics,* vol. 2. New York: North Holland, 1989.

Etounga-Manguellé, Daniel. *L'Afrique: A-t-elle besoin d'un programme d'ajustement culturel?* Ivry-sur-Seine: Editions Nouvelles du Sud, 1990.

Evenson, Robert, and Vishva Bindlish. "Impact Study of T&V Extension in Kenya." Agriculture and Rural Development Series no. 7. Washington, D.C.: Africa Technical Department, World Bank, 1993.

Evenson, Robert, and Mathurin Gbetibouo. "Impact Study of T&V Extension in Burkina Faso." Draft. Africa Technical Department, World Bank, 1993.

Falloux, François, and Lee Talbot. *Crise et opportunité: Environnement et développement en Afrique.* Paris: Editions G.-P. Maisonneuve & Larose, 1992.

Falloux, François, Lee Talbot, and Jeri Larson. "National Environmental Action Plans in Sub-Saharan Africa: Progress and Next Steps." Washington, D.C.: World Bank, 1991.

Federal Reserve Bank of Boston, sponsor. *The International Monetary System: Forty Years after Bretton Woods.* Proceedings of a conference held in May 1984 sponsored by the Federal Reserve Bank of Boston held at Bretton Woods, New Hampshire. Conference Series no. 28. Boston: Federal Reserve Bank of Boston, 1984.

Fischer, Stanley, and William Easterly. "The Economics of the Government Budget Constraint." *World Bank Research Observer* 5 (July 1990): 127–42.

Freeman, Gary P. "Can Liberal States Control Unwanted Migration?" In "Strategies for Immigration Control: An International Comparison," edited by Mark J. Miller. *Annals of the American Academy of Political and Social Science* 534 (July 1994).

Frischtak, Claudio, with Bita Hadjimichael and Ulrich Zachau. *Competition Policies for Industrializing Countries.* Policy and Research Series 7. Washington, D.C.: World Bank, 1989.

Fukuyama, Francis. *The End of History and the Last Man.* New York: The Free Press, 1992.

Gastil, Raymond. *Freedom in the World.* New York: Freedom House, 1989.

Gewirts, Carl. "Debt Is Rising, but Burden Is Lighter, OECD Says." *International Herald Tribune,* September 14, 1992, 7.

Gilder, George. "The Death of Telephony." *The Economist* 328(7828) (September 11–17, 1993): 75–78.

Gillies, David. "Human Rights, Democracy, and 'Good Governance': Stretching the World Bank's Policy Frontiers." Paper prepared for the President, International Centre for Human Rights and Democratic Development, Montreal, June 1, 1992. (A version of this paper was presented at the International Conference on Human Rights in a New World Order, Prague, Czech and Slovak Federal Republic, June 9–12, 1992.)

Global Coalition for Africa. "Reducing Military Expenditure in Africa." Document GCA/AC.2/04/4/92. Report presented at the Second Advisory Committee Meeting of the Global Coalition for Africa, Kampala, Uganda, May 8–9, 1992. Global Coalition for Africa, Washington, D.C.

Grootaert, Christiaan. "The Evolution of Welfare and Poverty during

Structural Change and Economic Recession—The Case of Côte d'Ivoire, 1985–1988." Draft. Africa Technical Department, World Bank, Washington, D.C., September 30, 1992.

Grosenick, Leigh E. "Research in Democratic Governance." *Public Administration Quarterly* (Fall 1984): 266–87.

Hawes, Hugh, and David Stephens. *Questions of Quality: Primary Education and Development.* Essex, United Kingdom: Longman Group, 1990.

Healey, Denis. *The Time of My Life.* New York: W. W. Norton Press, 1990.

Heller, Peter. "Fund-Supported Adjustment Programs and the Poor." *Finance & Development* 25 (4) (December 1988): 2–5.

Heller, Peter, and others. *The Implications of Fund-Supported Adjustment Programs for Poverty: Experiences in Selected Countries.* Occasional Paper no. 58. Washington, D.C.: International Monetary Fund, 1988.

Hemming, Richard, and Ali Mansoor. "Is Privatization the Answer?" *Finance & Development* 25 (3) (September 1988): 31–33.

Herz, Barbara K., and Shahidur R. Khandker, eds. *Women's Work, Education, and Family Welfare in Peru.* World Bank Discussion Paper no. 116. Washington, D.C.: World Bank, 1991.

Hicks, Ronald, and Odd Per Brekk. *Assessing the Impact of Structural Adjustment on the Poor: The Case of Malawi.* IMF Working Paper WP/91/112. Washington, D.C.: International Monetary Fund, November 1991.

Howe, Herbert M. "Military Integration in Zimbabwe, 1980." Address before the African Studies Association, Seattle, Wa., November 20, 1992. Office of the Director of African Studies, School of Foreign Service, Georgetown University, Washington, D.C., April 1992.

———. "National Reconciliation and a New South African Defense Force." Address before the Institute on African Affairs at the 1992 Conference on African Policy Issues, Washington, D.C., April 23, 1992. Office of the Director of African Studies, School of Foreign Service, Georgetown University, Washington, D.C., April 1992.

Humphreys, Charles, and William Jaeger. "Africa's Adjustment and Growth." *Finance & Development* 26 (2) (June 1989): 6–8.

Huntington, Samuel P. *Political Order in Changing Societies.* New Haven, Conn.: Yale University Press, 1968.

Huntington, Samuel P., and Joan Nelson. *No Easy Choice.* Cambridge: Harvard University Press, 1976.

Husain, Ishrat. "Adjustment and the Impact on the Poor: The Case of Africa." Paper presented to the Economic Data Institute Seminar at the African Development Bank, Abidjan, March 9–12, 1992. Office of the Chief Economist, Africa Region, World Bank, Washington, D.C.

———. "An Assessment of Structural Adjustment in Sub-Saharan

Africa." Paper prepared for the Council of African Advisers. Office of the Chief Economist, Africa Region, World Bank, Washington, D.C., September 29, 1992.

Husain, Ishrat, and John Underwood, eds. *African External Finance in the 1990s*. A World Bank Symposium. Washington, D.C.: World Bank, 1991.

Hyden, Goran. *No Shortcuts to Progress: African Development Management in Perspective*. Berkeley: University of California Press, 1983.

———. "The Changing Context of Institutional Development in Sub-Saharan Africa." In *Background Papers: The Long-Term Perspective Study of Sub-Saharan Africa*. Vol. 3, *Institutional and Sociopolitical Issues*. Washington, D.C.: World Bank, 1990.

"Immediate Release: Formation of the African Democratic League." *The African Mirror* 2 (10 and 11) (April/May 1992): 32–33.

Ingram, Gregory K. "Economic Development: Its Record and Determinants." In *CIOS XXI World Management Congress: Management Challenges for the 1990s; Program and Plenary Proceedings*. New York: North American Management Council, 1990.

Institute for Resource Development/Macro Systems, Inc. *Demographic and Health Survey 1988*. Columbia, Md.: Institute for Resource Development/Macro Systems, Inc., 1988.

International Currency Analysis, Inc., data. Brooklyn, N.Y., various years.

International Labour Organization and the World Employment Program. *African Employment Report 1990*. Addis Ababa: Jobs and Skills Program for Africa (JASPA), 1990.

International Monetary Fund. *Annual Report of the International Monetary Fund*. Washington, D.C.: International Monetary Fund, 1990.

———. *Directory of Economic, Commodity, and Development Organizations*. Washington, D.C.: International Monetary Fund, 1992.

International Monetary Fund, Bureau of Statistics. *Direction of Trade Statistics Yearbook 1987*. Washington, D.C.: International Monetary Fund, 1987.

———. *Direction of Trade Statistics Yearbook 1992*. Washington, D.C.: International Monetary Fund, 1992.

Jamal, Vali, and John Weeks. *Africa Misunderstood or Whatever Happened to the Rural-Urban Gap?* Macmillan and International Labour Office. Forthcoming.

Jay, K., and C. Michalopoulos. "Donor Policies, Donor Interests, and Aid Effectiveness." In *Aid and Development*, edited by Anne O. Krueger and Constantine Michalopoulos. Baltimore: Johns Hopkins University Press, 1989.

Jaycox, Edward V. K. "African External Finance in the 1990s." Remarks presented at Global Coalition for Africa Advisory Committee meeting,

Paris, September 10, 1991. Global Coalition for Africa, Washington, D.C.
———. "The Challenges of African Development." Washington, D.C.: World Bank, 1992.
———. "Comments on Africa's External Finance in the 1990s." Paper presented at Global Coalition for Africa Advisory Committee meeting, Kampala, Uganda, May 8–9, 1992. Global Coalition for Africa, Washington, D.C.
Jepma, Catinus. "The Tying of Aid." In *Development Centre Studies*. Paris: Organization for Economic Cooperation and Development, 1991.
Joint Ministerial Committee of the Boards of Governors of the World Bank and the International Monetary Fund on the Transfer of Real Resources to Developing Countries (Development Committee). "Resource Flows to Developing Countries." Issues paper prepared by World Bank and International Monetary Fund staff for consideration at the 44th meeting of the Development Committee, September 21, 1992.
Joseph, Richard. *Democracy and Prebendal Politics in Nigeria: The Rise and Fall of the Second Republic*. New York: Cambridge University Press, 1987; Ibadan: Spectrum Books, 1990.
Kabou, Axelle. *Et si l'Afrique refusait le développement?* Paris: L'Harmattan, 1991.
Kahnert, Friedrich. *Improving Urban Employment and Labor Productivity*. World Bank Discussion Paper no. 10. Washington, D.C.: World Bank, 1987.
Kaldor, Mary. "After the Cold War: Obstacles and Opportunities in Cutting Arms Budgets." In *Proceedings of the World Bank Annual Conference on Development Economics 1991*, 141–56. Washington, D.C.: World Bank, 1992.
Kanbur, Ravi. *Poverty and the Social Dimensions of Structural Adjustment in Côte d'Ivoire*. SDA Working Paper no. 2. Washington, D.C.: World Bank, 1990.
Kawakami, Takao. "Japan's ODA Policies for a Peace Initiative." Address presented at the Tokyo Conference on Arms Reduction and Economic Development in the Post–Cold War Era, Tokyo, November 5, 1992.
Keener, Sarah, Suzanne Heigh, Luiz Pereira da Silva, and Nicole Ball. "Demobilization and Reintegration of Military Personnel in Africa: The Evidence from Seven Country Case Studies." Africa Regional Series Report no. IDP–130. World Bank, Washington, D.C., October 1993.
Kikeri, Sunita, John Nellis, and Mary Shirley. *Privatization: The Lessons of Experience*. Washington, D.C.: World Bank, 1992.
King, Elizabeth, and M. Ann Hill, eds. *Women's Education in Developing Countries*. Baltimore: Johns Hopkins University Press, 1993.
Krueger, Anne O. "Aid in the Development Process." *World Bank Research*

Observer 1 (January 1986): 57–78.

Krueger, Anne O., and Constantine Michalopoulos, eds. *Aid and Development*. Baltimore: Johns Hopkins University Press, 1989.

Krueger, Anne O., and Vernon Ruttan. "The Development of Economic Assistance to LDCs." Economic Development Center, University of Minnesota, for the United States Agency for International Development and the Department of State, 1983.

Lake, Anthony, and contributors. *After the Wars: Reconstruction in Afghanistan, Indochina, Central America, Southern Africa, and the Horn of Africa*. U.S.–Third World Policy Perspectives no. 16. Washington, D.C.: Overseas Development Council, 1990.

Lamboray, Jean-Louis, and A. Edward Elmendorf. *Combatting AIDS and Other Sexually Transmitted Diseases in Africa: A Review of the World Bank's Agenda for Action*. World Bank Discussion Paper no. 181. Washington, D.C.: World Bank, 1992.

Landell-Mills, Joslin. *Helping the Poor: The IMF's New Facilities for Structural Adjustment*. Rev. ed. Washington, D.C.: External Relations Department, International Monetary Fund, 1992.

Landell-Mills, Pierre. "Governance, Cultural Change, and Empowerment." *The Journal of Modern African Studies* 30 (3) (1992): 543–67.

Landell-Mills, Pierre, and Ismail Serageldin. "Governance and the Development Process." *Finance & Development* 28 (3) (September 1991): 14–17.

————. "Governance and the External Factor." In *Proceedings of the World Bank Annual Conference on Development Economics 1991*, 303–20. Washington, D.C.: World Bank, 1992.

Lele, Uma. *Aid to African Agriculture: Lessons from Two Decades of Donors' Experience*. Baltimore and London: Johns Hopkins University Press, 1991.

Levin, Ann, Eduard Bos, and My T. Vu. *Africa Region Population Projections, 1992–93 Edition*. Washington, D.C.: World Bank, 1992.

————. "Africa Region Population Projections." Report. Population and Human Resources Department, World Bank, Washington, D.C, 1992.

Little, I. M. D. "Small Manufacturing Enterprises in Developing Countries." *World Bank Economic Review* 1 (2) (January 1987): 203–35.

Lockheed, Marlaine E., and Adriaan M. Verspoor; with others. *Improving Primary Education in Developing Countries*. New York: Oxford University Press, 1991.

Lopez, Ramon, and Vinod Thomas. "Imports and Growth in Africa." Policy Research Working Paper WPS 20. Washington, D.C.: Country Economics Department, World Bank, 1988.

Lubell, Harold. *The Informal Sector in the 1980s and 1990s.* Development Centre, Organization for Economic Cooperation and Development, 1991.

Lusigi, Walter J., comp. *Managing Protected Areas in Africa: Report from a Workshop on Protected Area Management in Africa, Mweka, Tanzania.* Paris: UNESCO–World Heritage Fund, 1992.

Mabogunje, Akin L. "A New Paradigm for Urban Development." In *Proceedings of the World Bank Annual Conference on Development Economics 1992,* 191–208. Washington, D.C.: World Bank, 1992.

MacGaffey, Janet. *The Real Economy of Zaire: The Contribution of Smuggling and Other Unofficial Activities to National Wealth.* Philadelphia: University of Pennsylvania Press, 1991.

Maddison, Angus. *The World Economy in the 20th Century.* Paris: Development Centre, Organization for Economic Cooperation and Development, 1989.

"Mainstreaming Women in Development in Different Settings." Report. OECD/DAC/WID Expert Group, Paris, 1992.

Mason, Edward S., and Robert E. Asher. *The World Bank since Bretton Woods.* Washington, D.C.: Brookings Institution, 1973.

Maxwell, Simon, and others. "Food Security in Developing Countries." *IDS Bulletin* 21 (3) (July 1990): 1–83.

McCleary, William. "Policy Implementation under Adjustment Lending." *Finance & Development* 26 (1) (March 1989): 32–34.

McNamara, Robert S. Address before the American Society of Newspaper Editors, Montreal, May 18, 1966. World Bank, Washington, D.C.

————. *Africa's Development Crisis: Agricultural Stagnation, Population Explosion, and Environmental Degradation.* Washington, D.C.: Global Coalition for Africa, 1991.

————. "Military Expenditure and Development." In *Proceedings of the World Bank Annual Conference on Development Economics 1991,* 95–125. Washington, D.C.: World Bank, 1992.

Meier, Gerald, and William Steel, eds. *Industrial Adjustment in Sub-Saharan Africa.* New York: Oxford University Press, 1989.

Meier, Gerald, and Dudley Seers, eds. *Pioneers in Development.* Second series. New York: Oxford University Press, 1987.

Michaely, Michael, Armeane Choksi, and Demetris Papageorgiou. "The Design of Trade Liberalization." *Finance & Development* 26 (1) (March 1989): 2–5.

Miller, Mark J., ed. "Strategies for Immigration Control: An International Comparison." *Annals of the American Academy of Political and Social Science* 534 (July 1994).

Mining Unit, Industry and Energy Division. *Strategy for African Mining.*

World Bank Technical Paper no. 181. Washington, D.C.: World Bank, 1992.

Ministério da Economia e Finanças, Republica da Guiné-Bissau. *Estudo de préviabilidade da promoçao e fomento da microempresa em Bissau.* Bissau: Ministério da Economia e Finanças, Republica da Guiné-Bissau, 1991.

Morrow, Lance. "Africa: The Scramble for Existence." *Time International* 140 (10) (September 7, 1992): 28–37.

Moser, Caroline O.N. "Gender Planning in the Third World: Meeting Practical and Strategic Gender Needs." *World Development* 17 (11) (1989): 1799–825.

Mosley, Paul, and others. "Aid, the Public Sector and the Market in LDCs." *Economic Journal* 97 (September 1987): 616–41.

Mosley, Paul, Jane Harrigan, and John Toye. *Aid and Power: The World Bank and Policy-Based Lending.* Vol. 2, *Case Studies.* London and New York: Routledge, 1991.

National Environmental Action Plan documents. Prepared by the Governments of Burkina Faso, Ghana, Lesotho, Madagascar, Mauritius, Nigeria, Rwanda, and the Seychelles, 1989–1992. Country Departments, Africa Region, World Bank.

Nazer, Hisham M. "Development of the Environment and the Environment for Development." *OPEC Bulletin* 24 (2) (February 1993): 6–7, 45.

Nelson, Joan M., with Stephanie J. Eglinton. *Encouraging Democracy: What Role for Conditioned Aid?* Policy Essay no. 4. Washington, D.C.: Overseas Development Council, 1992.

Nordic UN Project. *The United Nations in Development.* Final Report by the Nordic UN Project. Stockholm: Almqvist and Wiksell International, 1991.

Nowels, Larry Q., and Jonathan E. Sanford. "Arab Economic Aid Donors and Recipients: Trends in Aid Flows to the Middle East/North Africa, 1973–1989." CRS Report for Congress no. 91–476 F. Congressional Research Service, Library of Congress, Washington, D.C., June 10, 1991.

Nsouli, Saleh. "Structural Adjustment in Sub-Saharan Africa." *Finance & Development* 26 (3) (September 1989): 30–33.

Organization for Economic Cooperation and Development. *Geographical Distribution of Financial Flows to Developing Countries, 1985/88.* Paris: Organization for Economic Cooperation and Development, 1988.

Organization for Economic Cooperation and Development and Development Assistance Committee. *Development Cooperation: Efforts and Policies of the Members of the Development Assistance Committee; 1991 Report.* Paris: Organization for Economic Cooperation and Development, 1991.

Osmanczyk, Edmund Jan. *The Encyclopedia of the United Nations and*

International Agreements. 2nd ed. New York: Taylor and Francis, 1990.

Over, Mead. "The Macroeconomic Impact of AIDS in Sub-Saharan Africa." Population, Health and Nutrition Technical Working Paper no. 3. Washington, D.C.: Africa Technical Department, World Bank, 1992.

Palmer, Ingrid. "Gender and Population in the Adjustment of African Economies: Planning for Change." *Women, Work and Development Series,* no. 19. Geneva: International Labour Office, 1991.

Paul, Samuel, David Steedman, and Francis Sutton. "Building Capacity for Policy Analysis." Policy, Planning and Research Working Paper WPS 220. Washington, D.C.: Country Economics Department, World Bank, 1989.

Pennock, J. Roland. "Rights, Natural Rights, and Human Rights: A General View." In *Human Rights: Nomos XXIII,* edited by J. Roland Pennock and John W. Chapman, 1–28. New York: New York University, 1981.

Peterson, George E., G. Thomas Kingsley, and Jeffrey P. Telgarsky. "Rethinking the Role of Urban Areas in National Economic Development." Chap. 1 in *Urban Economies and National Development.* Washington, D.C.: Urban Institute and Office of Housing and Urban Programs, United States Agency for International Development, 1991.

Poats, Rutherford. *Twenty-Five Years of Development Cooperation—A Review: Efforts and Policies of the Members of the Development Assistance Committee.* Paris: Organization for Economic Cooperation and Development, 1985.

Putnam, Robert D. "Social Capital and Public Affairs." *The American Prospect,* no. 13 (Spring 1993): 1–8.

Putnam, Robert D., with Robert Leonardi and Raffaella Y. Nanetti. *Making Democracy Work: Civic Traditions in Modern Italy.* Princeton, N.J.: Princeton University Press, 1993.

Ribe, Helena, and others. *How Adjustment Programs Can Help the Poor— The World Bank's Experience.* World Bank Discussion Paper no. 71. Washington, D.C.: World Bank, 1990.

Salmen, Lawrence F. *Reducing Poverty: An Institutional Perspective.* Poverty and Social Policy Series. Paper no. 1 (Program Design and Implementation). Washington, D.C.: World Bank, 1992.

Salome, Bernard, ed. *Fighting Urban Unemployment in Developing Countries.* Organization for Economic Cooperation and Development Centre Seminars. Paris: Organization for Economic Cooperation and Development, 1989.

Schafgans, Marcia. "Household Allocations in Kenya." Women in Development Division, Population and Human Resources Department, World Bank, Washington, D.C., August 1991.

Schiavone, Giuseppe. *International Organizations: A Dictionary and Directory*, 2nd ed. London: St. James Press, 1986.

Schloss, Miguel. *Does Downstream Petroleum Trade Matter?* Industry and Energy Division Note no. 14. Washington, D.C.: Africa Technical Department, World Bank, 1992.

Schmitz, Gerald J., and David Gillies. *The Challenge of Democratic Development: Sustaining Democratization in Developing Societies.* Ottawa: The North-South Institute, 1992.

Schultz, T. Paul. "The Relationship between Local Family Planning Expenditures and Fertility in Thailand, 1976–81." Center Discussion Paper no. 662. Economic Growth Center, Yale University, New Haven, Conn., April 1992.

Schumacher, E. F. *Small Is Beautiful.* New York: Perennial Library, 1989.

Selowsky, Marcelo. "Stages in the Recovery of Latin America's Growth." *Finance & Development* 27 (2) (June 1990): 28–31.

Sen, Amartya K. "Poverty: An Ordinal Approach to Measurement." *Econometrica* 44 (2) (March 1976): 219–31.

———. *Collective Choice and Social Welfare.* San Francisco: Holden/Day Publishing, 1970; North Holland, N.Y.: Elsevier Science Publishing, 1979.

———. *Poverty and Famines: An Essay on Entitlement and Deprivation.* Oxford: Clarendon Press, 1981.

———. *Resources, Values, and Development.* Cambridge: Harvard University Press, 1984.

———. "Values, Capability and Well-Being in Development Assistance." Paper presented to the SIDA Workshop on Development Assistance from the Perspective of Recipient Countries, Stockholm, April 26–28, 1989.

———. "Women's Survival as a Development Problem." Comments prepared for the 1700th Stated Meeting of the American Academy of Arts and Sciences, March 8, 1989.

———. "International Freedom as a Social Commitment," *The New York Review of Books* 37 (10) (June 14, 1990): 49–55.

———. "More than 100 Million Women Are Missing." *The New York Review of Books* 37 (20) (December 20, 1990): 61–66.

Serageldin, Ismail. "The Contributions of Arab Aid Agencies and the Need for Strengthening Working Relations with Them." Paper. Office of the Vice President, Environmentally Sustainable Development, World Bank, Washington, D.C., September 23, 1990.

———. *Development Partners: Aid and Cooperation in the 1990s.* Office of the Vice President, Environmentally Sustainable Development, World

Bank, Washington, D.C., 1993.

———. "Governance, Democracy and the World Bank in Africa." Office of the Vice President, Environmentally Sustainable Development, World Bank, Washington, D.C., September 20, 1990.

———. "Military Spending in Developing Countries," *Bank's World* 9 (6) (June 1990): 10–11.

———. "The Social Dimensions of Adjustment in Africa: A Policy Overview." Paper presented at the Second Annual International Conference on Socio-Economics, Washington, D.C., March 16–18, 1990. Office of the Vice President, Environmentally Sustainable Development, World Bank, Washington, D.C.

———. *Saving Africa's Rainforests*. 2nd ed. Washington, D.C.: World Bank, 1993.

———. "Subsidies: Who Pays and Who Benefits?" *Al-Ahram* (November 14, 1991): 4.

———. "The Challenge of a Holistic Vision: Culture, Empowerment, and the Development Paradigm." In *Culture and Development in Africa: Proceedings of an International Conference*, edited by Ismail Serageldin and June Taboroff, 15–32. Washington, D.C.: World Bank, 1993.

———. "Investing in Africa: The World Bank's Program of Assistance and Opportunities for the Private Sector." Industry and Energy Division Note no. 9. Africa Technical Department, World Bank, Washington, D.C., January 1992.

———. "Mirrors and Windows." Parts I and II. *Litterae* (Review of the European Academy of Sciences and Arts) 3(2–3)(Oct./Nov. 1993): 4–15 and 4(1)(1994): 8–26. Also in the *American Journal of Islamic Social Studies* 11(1)(Spring 1994): 79–107.

———. "Our Common Humanity: The Crisis of Values in Contemporary Society." *EAIE Newsletter* 13 (February 1994):3–10. Keynote address to the Fifth Annual Conference of the European Association for International Education, The Hague, December 2, 1993. Office of the Vice President, Environmentally Sustainable Development, World Bank, Washington, D.C.

———. "Public Administration in the 1990s: Rising to the Challenge." In *Public Administration in the Nineties: Trends and Innovations*. Proceedings of the XXIInd International Congress of Administrative Sciences. Brussels: International Institute of Administrative Sciences, 1992.

Serageldin, Ismail, A. Edward Elmendorf, and El-Tigani E. El-Tigani. "Structural Adjustment and Health in Africa in the 1980s." In *Research in Human Capital and Development*, edited by Alan Sarkin and Ismail Sirageldin. Vol. 8, *Nutrition, Development, and Public Policy*. Greenwich,

Conn.: JAI Press, forthcoming.

Serageldin, Ismail, and Pierre Landell-Mills. "Governance and the Development Process." *Finance & Development* 28 (3) (September 1991): 14–17.

Serageldin, Ismail, Adewale Sangowawa, and Ahmedou Ould-Abdallah. "African Development: Diagnosis and Recommendations." In *Africa: Rise to Challenge—Towards a Conference on Security, Stability, Development and Cooperation in Africa* edited by Olusegun Obasanjo and Felix G. N. Mosha. Abeokuta, Nigeria: Africa Leadership Forum, 1993.

Serageldin, Ismail, and Pierre Landell-Mills, eds. *Overcoming Global Hunger: Proceedings of a Conference on Actions to Reduce Poverty and Hunger Worldwide.* Environmentally Sustainable Development Proceedings Series no. 3. Washington, D.C.: World Bank, 1994.

Serageldin, Ismail, and Andrew Steer, eds. *Making Development Sustainable: From Concepts to Action.* Environmentally Sustainable Development Occasional Paper Series No. 2. Washington, D.C.: World Bank, 1994.

Serageldin, Ismail, and Andrew Steer, eds. *Valuing the Environment: Proceedings of the First Annual International Conference on Environmentally Sustainable Development.* Environmentally Sustainable Development Proceedings Series no. 2. Washington, D.C.: World Bank, 1994.

Serageldin, Ismail, and June Taboroff, eds. *Culture and Development in Africa: Proceedings of an International Conference.* Environmentally Sustainable Development Proceedings Series No. 1. Washington, D.C.: World Bank, 1994.

Service des Affaires financières et de la Coordination géographique, Ministère de la Coopération et du Développement. *Les Etats d'Afrique, de l'océan Indien et des Caraïbes: Situation économique et financière en 1990/Perspectives d'évolution en 1991–1992.* Ministère de la Coopération et du Développement, 1991.

Shafik, Nemat, and Sushenjit Bandyopadhyay. "Economic Growth and Environmental Quality: Time Series and Cross-Country Evidence." Background paper for *World Development Report 1992: Development and the Environment.* Policy Research Working Paper WPS 904. Washington, D.C.: Office of the Vice President, Development Economics, World Bank, 1992.

Sharma, Narendra, ed. *Managing the World's Forests: Looking for Balance between Conservation and Development.* Dubuque, Iowa: Kendall/Hunt Publishing Company, 1992.

Sherbiny, Naiem. *Arab Financial Institutions and Developing Countries.* World Bank Staff Working Paper no. 794. Washington, D.C.: World Bank, 1986.

Shihata, Ibrahim F. I. *The Other Face of OPEC: Financial Assistance to the Third World, Energy Resources and Policies of the Middle East and North Africa.* London and New York: Longman, 1982.

————. "The World Bank and Human Rights: An Analysis of the Legal Issues and the Record of Achievements." Paper submitted to the Third World Legal Studies Association Panel on the World Bank, Development Projects and Human Rights: The Obligations of the Bank, Miami, January 8, 1988. Office of the General Counsel, World Bank, Washington, D.C.

————. "Issues of 'Governance' in Borrowing Members: The Extent of Their Relevance under the Bank's Articles of Agreement." Memorandum of the Vice President and General Counsel. Office of the General Counsel, World Bank, Washington, D.C., December 21, 1990.

————. *The World Bank in a Changing World: Selected Essays.* Compiled and edited by Franziska Tschofen and Antonio R. Parra. Dordrecht, the Netherlands: Martinus Nijhoff Publishers, 1991.

Shihata, Ibrahim F.I., and others. *The OPEC Fund for International Development: The Formative Years.* New York: St. Martin's Press, 1983.

Sivard, Ruth Leger. *World Military and Social Expenditures 1991.* 14th ed. Washington, D.C.: World Priorities, 1991.

Sivard, Ruth Leger, Arlette Brauer, and Milton I. Roemer. *World Military and Social Expenditures 1989.* 13th ed. Washington, D.C.: World Priorities, 1989.

South Commission. *The Challenge to the South: The Report of the South Commission.* New York: Oxford University Press, 1990.

Soyinka, Wole. "Culture, Memory, and Development." In *Culture and Development in Africa: Proceedings of an International Conference,* interim document, edited by Ismail Serageldin and June Taboroff, 205–22. Washington, D.C.: Africa Technical Department, World Bank, 1992.

Spirer, Herbert F. "Violations of Human Rights—How Many? The Statistical Problems of Measuring Such Infractions Are Tough, but Statistical Science Is Equal to It." *American Journal of Economics and Sociology* 48 (1989): 199–210.

Squire, Lyn, and Herman G. van der Tak. *Economic Analysis of Projects.* Baltimore: Johns Hopkins Press, 1975.

Steel, William. "Adjusting Industrial Policy in Sub-Saharan Africa." *Finance & Development* 25 (1) (March 1988): 36–39.

Steer, Andrew. "The Environment for Development." *Finance & Development* 29 (2) (June 1992): 18–21.

"Structural Adjustment: Concessional Facilities Assist Low-Income Countries," *IMF Survey: Supplement on the International Monetary Fund,* September 1992: 19.

Summers, Lawrence H. *The Challenge of Development: Some Lessons of History for Sub-Saharan Africa.* Nigerian Institute of International Affairs Lecture Series no. 74. Lagos: Nigerian Institute of International Affairs, 1992.

————. "The Challenges of Development: Some Lessons of History for

Sub-Saharan Africa." *Finance & Development* 29 (1) (March 1992): 6–9.

———. "Investing in *All* the People." Policy Research Working Paper WPS 905. Washington, D.C.: Office of the Vice President and Chief Economist, World Bank, 1992.

Thomas, Vinod, and Ajay Chhibber. "Experience with Policy Reforms under Adjustment." *Finance & Development* 26 (1) (March 1989): 28–31.

United Nations Children's Fund. *The Invisible Adjustment: Poor Women and the Economic Crisis.* 2nd ed. Santiago: Women in Development, Regional Program, UNICEF, 1989.

———. *1992 UNICEF Annual Report.* New York: United Nations Children's Fund, 1992.

United Nations Development Programme. *Human Development Report 1990.* New York: Oxford University Press, 1990.

———. *Human Development Report 1991.* New York: Oxford University Press, 1991.

———. *Human Development Report 1992.* New York: Oxford University Press, 1992.

———. *S.M.A.R.T. Profiles: Socio-economic Monetary and Resource Tables.* New York: Resources Mobilization Unit, United Nations Development Programme, 1991.

———. *African Futures: The Preparation of National Long-Term Perspective Studies (NLTPS).* UNDP Regional Project RAF/91/006. New York: United Nations Development Programme, 1992.

United Nations Development Programme and the World Bank. *African Development Indicators.* Washington, D.C.: World Bank, 1992.

United Nations General Assembly. The Universal Declaration of Human Rights. Adopted and proclaimed by UN General Assembly Resolution 217 (III), December 10, 1948.

———. The International Covenant on Civil and Political Rights. Adopted and opened for signature, ratification, and accession by UN General Assembly Resolution 2200 A (XI), December 16, 1966. 21 UN GAO Supp. (No. 16). UN Doc. A/6316 (1967).

———. The International Covenant on Economic, Social and Cultural Rights. Adopted and opened for signature, ratification, and accession by UN General Assembly Resolution 2200 A (XI), December 16, 1966. 21 U.N. GAO Supp. (No. 16). UN Doc. A/6316 (1967).

Van den Boogaerde, Pierre. *Financial Assistance from Arab Countries and Arab Regional Institutions.* Occasional Paper no. 87. Washington, D.C.: International Monetary Fund, 1991.

Van Wijnbergen, Sweder. "Macro-Economic Aspects of the Effectiveness of Foreign Aid: On the Two-Gap Model, Home Goods Disequilibrium and Real Exchange Rate Misalignment." Discussion Paper, Report no.

DRD112. Development Research Department, World Bank, Washington, D.C., September 1984.

Verspoor, Adriaan. *Pathways to Change: Improving the Quality of Education in Developing Countries.* World Bank Discussion Paper no. 53. Washington, D.C.: World Bank, 1989.

Von Braun, Joachim, and others. "Improving Household Food Security." A "Theme Paper" in preparation for the FAO/WHO International Conference on Nutrition, IFPRI, Washington, D.C., October 1991.

Vu, My T., Eduard Bos, and Ann Levin. "Europe and Central Asia Region/Middle East and North Africa Region Population Projections, 1992–93 Edition." Policy Research Working Paper no. 1016. Washington, D.C.: World Bank, 1992.

————. "Latin America and the Caribbean Region (and Northern America) Population Projections, 1992–93 Edition." Policy Research Working Paper no. 1033. Washington, D.C.: World Bank, 1992.

Wahba, Sadek, and John Whalley. "Designing a Sustainable Macro-Analytic Capacity Building Program: The Example of Côte d'Ivoire." Paper. Africa Technical Department, World Bank, Washington, D.C., 1992.

Wai, Dunstan M. "Governance, Economic Development and the Role of External Actors." Paper delivered at the Conference on "Governance and Economic Development in Sub-Saharan Africa," Oxford University, May 2–4, 1991. External Affairs Office, Africa Region, World Bank, Washington, D.C.

Webster's New Collegiate Dictionary. Springfield, Mass.: Merriam-Webster, Inc., 1975.

Wheeler, Joseph C. "The Critical Role for Official Development Assistance in the 1990s." *Finance & Development* 26 (3) (September 1989): 38–40.

————. *Development Cooperation in the 1990s: Efforts and Policies of the Members of the Development Assistance Committee; 1989 Report.* Paris: Organization for Economic Cooperation and Development, 1989.

World Bank. *World Development Report 1983.* New York: Oxford University Press.

————. "Toward Sustained Development: A Joint Program of Action for Sub-Saharan Africa." Report no. PUB 5228. 2 vols. Washington, D.C.: World Bank, 1984.

————. *The Challenge of Hunger in Africa: A Call to Action.* Washington, D.C.: World Bank, 1988.

————. *Education in Sub-Saharan Africa: Policies for Adjustment, Revitalization, and Expansion.* Washington, D.C: World Bank, 1988.

————. *Sub-Saharan Africa: From Crisis to Sustainable Growth; A Long-Term Perspective Study.* Washington, D.C.: World Bank, 1989.

————. *Successful Development in Africa: Case Studies of Projects, Programs, and Policies.* Economic Development Institute (EDI) Development Policy Case Series, Analytical Case Studies no. 1. Washington, D.C.: World Bank, 1989.

―――. *World Debt Tables 1989–90: External Debt of Developing Countries.* Vol. 2, *Country Tables.* Washington, D.C.: World Bank, 1989.

―――. *How the World Bank Works with Nongovernmental Organizations.* Washington, D.C.: World Bank, 1990.

―――. *World Development Report 1990: Poverty.* New York: Oxford University Press, 1990.

―――. *The African Capacity Building Initiative: Toward Improved Policy Analysis and Development Management.* Washington, D.C.: World Bank, 1991.

―――. *World Debt Tables 1991–92: External Debt of Developing Countries.* Vol. 1, *Analysis and Summary Tables.* Washington, D.C.: World Bank, 1991.

―――. *World Development Report 1991: The Challenge of Development.* New York: Oxford University Press, 1991.

―――. "Financial Flows to Developing Countries: Current Developments." Quarterly review. Debt and International Finance Division, World Bank, September 1992.

―――. *Global Economic Prospects and the Developing Countries 1992.* Washington, D.C.: World Bank, 1992.

―――. *Poverty Reduction Handbook.* Washington, D.C.: World Bank, 1992.

―――. "Promoting Girls' Education: A Key to Development in the Sahel." Paper. Population and Human Resources Division, Sahelian Department, World Bank, Washington, D.C., September 1992.

―――. "Strategic Agenda for Private Sector Development— Confronting Challenges on Sub-Saharan Africa." Industry and Energy Division Note no. 11. Africa Technical Department, World Bank, Washington, D.C., 1992.

―――. *The World Bank and the Environment: 1992.* Washington, D.C.: World Bank, 1992.

―――. *The World Bank Annual Report 1992.* Washington, D.C.: World Bank, 1992.

―――. *World Debt Tables 1992–93: External Debt of Developing Countries.* Vol. 1, *Analysis and Summary Tables.* Washington, D.C.: World Bank, 1992.

―――. *World Debt Tables 1992–93: External Debt of Developing Countries.* Vol. 2, *Country Tables.* Washington, D.C.: World Bank, 1992.

―――. *World Development Report 1992: Development and the Environment.* New York: Oxford University Press, 1992.

―――. *World Development Report 1993: Investing in Health.* New York: Oxford University Press, 1993.

————. "Resettlement and Development: The Bankwide Review of Projects Involving Involuntary Resettlement 1986–1993." Environment Department, World Bank, Washington, D.C., April 1994.

————. "United Nations Children's Fund (UNICEF)." Background information. Operations Policy Unit, Central Operations Department, World Bank, Washington, D.C., no date.

World Bank and the World Food Programme. "Food Aid in Africa: An Agenda for the 1990s." Joint study. Washington, D.C., and Rome, August 1991.

World Conference on Education for All. "Meeting Basic Learning Needs." Final report of conference held March 5–9, 1990, Jomtien, Thailand. New York, 1990.

Xiao, Geng. "Managerial Autonomy, Fringe Benefits, and Ownership Structure: A Comparative Study of Chinese State and Collective Enterprises." *China Economic Review* 2 (1) (1991): 47–73.

Acronyms and Abbreviations

AFTIM	Africa Technical Department, Institutional Development and Management Division (now Capacity Building Division), World Bank
AIDS	Acquired immune deficiency syndrome
AKRSP	Aga Khan Rural Support Programme
CEC	Commission of European Communities
CG	Consultative Group
CGIAR	Consultative Group on International Agricultural Research
CIDA	Canadian International Development Agency
CIS	Commonwealth of Independent States
CSSDCA	Conference on Peace, Security, Stability, Development and Cooperation in Africa
DAC	Development Assistance Committee
DEP	Development Economics Research Programme
DRS	Debt Reporting Service
EBRD	European Bank for Reconstruction and Development
EC	European Community
ECOSOC	Economic and Social Council of the United Nations
EDI	Economic Development Institute of the World Bank
ESD	Environmentally Sustainable Development
FAO	Food and Agriculture Organization of the United Nations
FDI	Foreign Direct Investment
GCA	Global Coalition for Africa
GDP	Gross domestic product

GEF	Global Environment Facility
GNP	Gross national product
GTZ	Deutsche Gesellschaft für Technische Zusammenarbeit
HDI	Human Development Index
HFI	Human Freedom Index
HRD	Human resource development
ICB	International competitive bidding
IDA	International Development Association
IDS	Institute of Development Studies
IFC	International Finance Corporation
IFI	International financial institution
IMF	International Monetary Fund
I.R.	Islamic Republic
IRP	Integrated Roads Project (Tanzania)
IUCN	International Union for the Conservation of Nature and Natural Resources (now World Conservation Union)
JASPA	Jobs and Skills Program for Africa
LCB	Local competitive bidding
MOW	Ministry of Works (Tanzania)
NARS	National agricultural research systems
NGO	Nongovernmental organization
NLTPS	National Long-Term Perspective Study
NRSP	National Rural Support Programme (Pakistan)
NTPC	National Thermal Power Corporation (India)
NWFP	North-Western Frontier Province (Pakistan)
ODA	Official development assistance; Overseas Development Administration (U.K.)
OECD	Organization for Economic Cooperation and Development
OPEC	Organization of Petroleum Exporting Countries
PAPSCA	Programme for the Alleviation of Poverty and the

	Social Costs of Adjustment (Uganda)
P.D.R.	People's Democratic Republic
PFP	Policy Framework Paper
REO	Regional Engineer's Office (Tanzania)
SDA	Social Dimensions of Adjustment
SDR	Special drawing right
SIDA	Swedish International Development Authority
SIRP	Social Infrastructure Relief Project
S.M.A.R.T.	Socio-economic Monetary and Resource Tables
SOE	State-owned enterprise
SPA	Special Program of Assistance for Africa
SSA	Sub-Saharan Africa
T&V	Training and Visit system
UN	United Nations
UNCED	United Nations Conference on Environment and Development
UNDP	United Nations Development Programme
UNESCO	United Nations Educational, Scientific, and Cultural Organization
UNICEF	United Nations Children's Fund
USSR	Union of Soviet Socialist Republics
WHO	World Health Organization
WID	Women in Development
WPS	Working Paper Series